John Arthur Fraser

A delicate Question

An original comedy Drama in four Acts

John Arthur Fraser

A delicate Question
An original comedy Drama in four Acts

ISBN/EAN: 9783337054960

Printed in Europe, USA, Canada, Australia, Japan

Cover: Foto ©ninafisch / pixelio.de

More available books at **www.hansebooks.com**

AUTHOR'S EDITION.

A· DELICATE QUESTION

An Original Comedy Drama

IN FOUR ACTS

BY

J. A. FRASER, Jr.

Author of A Noble Outcast- The Train Wreckers- Edelweiss
--McGinty's Troubles-- Linked by Law—The Judge's
Wife--Under an Alias—Modern Ananias--The
New State's Attorney—Face to Face—
'Twixt Love and Money--The
Merry Cobbler—etc.

CHICAGO.
THE DRAMATIC PUBLISHING COMPANY.

Characters.

Ezra Meeker—*The Henpecked.*
"Mariar"—*The Henpecker.*
Zachariah Smarden—*The Reformer.*
Will Goodall—*The Hired Man.*
Elsie Meeker—*The Choir Leader.*
Harry Meeker—*The Black Sheep.*
Lem Davis—*The Saloon Keeper.*
Ben Spraddling—*The Mayor.*
Tom Barton—*The Police Force.*
Jaggsy—*The Town "Bum."*
Seth Soper—*The Postmaster.*
Pickles—*The Bound Girl.*

ACT I.
The Question discussed with frankness. Meeker's door yard.

ACT II.
The Question agitated with fervor. Meeker's kitchen.

ACT III.
The Question handled with force. Lem's saloon.

ACT IV.
The Question settled with firmness. Home, Sweet Home.

Plays two hours. Time—The present day. Place—Iowa.

NOTE.—*This piece may be played with five men and three women by doubling* (1) *Harry Meeker and Jaggsy, Tom Barton and Ben Spraddling:* (2) *Lem Davis and Seth Soper:* (3) *Zach., Lem and Will going on for whitecaps.*

Supers will, of course, add to the effectiveness of the stage pictures.

Notes on Production.

A Delicate Question will be found one of the most successful comedies ever played by amateurs. The leading characters are not only easily acted but they are so evenly balanced that only superior ability can determine which the audience will most admire. Back of all the fun an interesting and pathetic story is told, which holds the eager attention till the last word. The question discussed in the play—the saloon question—is one which is uppermost in every community. The moral is pointed without a line of preaching, and is as irresistable as it is amusingly developed. The management of the stage is given in complete detail, and the labor of rehearsal, for this reason, will be found materially lightened. Every actor can see at a glance his position at every movement of the performance. The scenery is easy to handle, all the settings being simple, and the one sensational effect is easy to manage. The costumes are everyday clothes such as everybody has.

Costumes.

Ezra. First act—Old jeans pants, calico shirt, heavy top boots and battered old "cowfeed" straw hat. Half bald, grey wig, grey chin piece. Act 2—Well worn, ill-fitting suit, white collar and black tie. While off during the skunk incident he changes pants and tucks them up, reappearing with undershirt and in a barrel. He then puts on shirt and different coat and slippers. At close of act appears with night gown hanging out of pants behind. Act 3—Same coat and pants as in Act 2, with slouch felt hat. Act 4—Same. **Maria.** Old-fashioned black skirt, gaudy hat, old-fashioned wrap and sunshade. Act 2 Calico dress and apron. Act 3—Same as act 1. Act 4—Another calico dress and same hat. **Zachariah.** Black suit of ministerial cut, white choker, silk hat, black gloves. He is made up pale and clean shaven, with beard showing beneath the skin. Black wig parted in the middle and slicked down close to his head. Same dress all through. **Will.** Act 1—Overalls, calico shirt, no coat, old felt hat. Acts 2, 3, and 4 dark, neat suit with round "granger" felt hat. **Elsie.** Pretty walking dress, change to pretty calico wrapper. Act 2 Neat house dress, which may be worn all through. **Harry.** Smart, stylish business suit, but rather loud. **Lem.** Very flashy clothing, soft felt hat, no collar. In act 3 he is in his shirt sleeves with white apron on. Wears large diamond (?) in shirt, but no collar or tie. Clean shaved except small black chin beard. **Spraddling.** A little, weak-looking old man. White wig, dark suit, silk hat, black tie, white side whiskers. **Tom Barton.** Rough suit, policeman's helmet, large star on coat and carries a stout stick. **Jaggsy.** Tramp make-up, ragged, with stubble of beard and red nose. Second dress a little more respectable. **Seth.** Very bald, white wig, spectacles, dark suit. **Pickles.** Act 1—Ragged calico dress, knee skirt, shoes unbuttoned, very untidy. Act 2—Much neater calico dress and pinafore. Same in Act 3. Somewhat "dressed up" in Act 4.

Property Plot.

ACT I. Small rough bench; pump or well box with pail of of water beside it, or pail may stand on bench under window; tin dipper; Set tree; garden seat; picket fence; law book for Bill; slapsticks to be used off R. when Maria is beating Ezra and Pickles; crockery crash; set of harness; two written letters for Jaggsy in envelopes; coin for Elsie in pocket book; tin dishpan with potatoes in it; pot stick for Maria.

ACT II. Kitchen table; kitchen dresser with drawer and dishes; small, plain table; ironing board; rough dry and ironed washing; flat irons and holder; clothes basket and horse; checker board and checkers; valise and clothing to put in it; patent rocking chair and five common chairs; cash box; roll of paper money for Lem, also bill heads; letter for Ezra; double barreled gun; black snake whip for white caps. NOTE: One is a dummy made of black cloth stuffed with hay, and with a lash of plaited cotton cloth for Ezra to use. The sound is given by some one whipping behind the scene. Sugar barrel with bottom out; lighted lamp on small table; lighted dark lantern for whitecaps; lighted stable lantern for Pickles; wallet for Zachariah to put money in, also umbrella and bunch of keys; bunch of keys for Ezra; white hood masks for white caps; wallet for Will with paper money in it.

ACT III. Sign, "Cigars—LEM DAVIS—Billiards"; garden bench; beer kegs and barrels; coin for Jaggsy; bungstarter with padded head for Lem; paper package to represent dynamite cartridge with real fuse to light; steel bars, suspended by a string, and hammer to beat them to immitate fire bells. NOTE: For the explosion use a tomato can with gunpowder at bottom, led to by short fuse, and filled up with gunpowder and sawdust; fire it in entrance and at the same time fire a gun into an empty barrel and light red fire inside house; have bricks and old plaster on a trip board above the entrance in which saloon is set and trip the stuff onto stage when the explosion occurs. This is easy to do and highly effective.

ACT IV. Newspaper; lighted lamp on table; basin with water and sponge; cotton bandage; fireman's ax.

A DELICATE QUESTION.

ACT I.

[*Exterior of the Meeker homestead. Set house* R. 2 E. *with prac. window and door. Supposed to be the back yard. Small bench* R. *Pump or well box* L. *Set tree with seat underneath* C. *opposite* 2. *Set barn* L. 3 E. (*or fake it*) *steps up to door of house. Picket fence across back with gate* C. *Landscape backing. Time: early afternoon in June. At rise* **Will** *is reading law book on bench* R.

Will. [*Reading.*] "Law is the perfection of reason; it always intends to conform thereto, and that which is not reason is not law. Justinian reduces the whole doctrine of law to these three general principles: Live honestly, hurt nobody, and render to everyone his just due." If Mrs. Meeker only lived up to that last principle she would have dinner ready, instead of gadding off to a noonday meeting. [*Voices heard off* L. C. E.] Hello, she's coming now. [**Maria** *with* **Zachariah** *and* **Elsie** *with* **Deacon** *enter* L. C. E. *cross to* C. *and come down.*]

Mar. [*Speaking as she enters.*] As you said this mornin', Brother Smarden, the whole liquor trade had ought to be swept offen the face of the earth, and them that persists in sellin' the stuff had ought to go to penitentiary. [*This brings her down* L. *with* **Zach.** **Elsie** *sits* C. *in conversation with* **Deacon** *and* **Will**, *who, after greetings, returns to his book.*]

Zach. Nothing but the most drastic measures, Sister Meeker, will rid the world of this awful curse. Ah! if the cause only had the support of more earnest, Christian women like yourself, we would then——

Mar. [*As she sees* **Bill.**] Well, I declare! Say, you, Bill! Do you think you git $20 a month and board for moonin' and mawkin' over books day and night?

Will. [*On bench* R. *Rising.*] This is my dinner hour, Mrs. Meeker. There was no dinner ready, so I thought I would fill in the time to advantage. [*Goes* C. *to* **Elsie.** **Zach.** *crosses and sits on bench* R.]

Mar. Huh! Couldn't a got Pickles to give you a snack, I suppose? [*Calls.*] Pickles! Pickles! [**Zach** *goes to* **Deacon** C.]

Pickles. [*Within.*] Yes, mum; I'm coming.

Mar. You'd better come a-runnin'. [*Crossing to door.*]

Elsie. Don't mind it, Will, it's only her way.

Will. Her way seems to be to make everybody as uncomfortable as she can. She succeeds in my case. I'm hungry.

Mar. [*Aside. Looking at* **Will** *and* **Elsie.** **Deacon** *talking to* **Zach.**] I'll put a stop to that business. No hired man for my gal. [*Aloud.*] Elsie, go in the house and see what's keepin' that dawdlin' little imp.

Elsie. Yes, mother. [*Ex. into house.* **Will** *starts to follow her.*]

Mar. [*Stopping him.*] They hain't no call for you to go in till dinner is ready. You can go to the barn and hunt eggs, and see that you don't suck none of them, neither.

Will. You seem to go out of your way to insult me to-day. [*Ex.* L. U. E.]

Mar. [*Down* C.] Don't you sass me back, young man, or you'll see trouble. [**Pickles** *appears at door.*] Why didn't you git dinner when you see they was a protracted meetin'?

Pickles. I didn't see no protracted meetin', and I wouldn't know what it was if I did see it. I ain't got my work done up, anyway.

Mar. Why, you lazy, shiftless, disobedient young monkey— you didn't have a thing to do, har'ly. [**Pickles** *crosses to* L. **Mar.** *follows.*] What was you doin'?

Pick. Made the beds, emptied the slops, fed the chickens, washed the dishes, scrubbed the kitchen, dusted the parlor, cleaned the stove, and now I'm learnin' the temperance pledge off by heart. Say, I wish you'd send me back to the poor house, so I could git a vacation.

Mar. Go right in and start a fire and then peel the pertatoes. Git a move onto you. Scat! [*Ex.* **Pickles** *into house.*] I'd ast you folks to stop to dinner, only they ain't anything in the house fit to eat, har'ly. I've been so powerful interested in the reform wave that I kinder had to let my housekeepin' slide.

Zach. Don't mention it, Sister Meeker. Deacon Soper and I were just discussing what is to be done about your husband. As he is one of the biggest taxpayers in town, and owns the building where Lem Davis keeps saloon, it makes it all the harder to have him against the Lord's side.

Deacon. Especially as Sister Smarden is so liberal to the church and foreign missions. Cash counts these times. [*He and* **Zach.** *rise.*]

Mar. You're not goin', be you. [R. C.]

Zach. There is work in the vineyard, Sister Meeker, and we must move along. Now *do* use all your influence with your husband. We must rid our fair town of this accursed traffic—it is the Lord's work, sister.

Mar. You leave Ezra to me and the Lord, Brother Smarden. It'll be mighty hard sleddin', but we'll convert Ezra.

Ezra. [*Sticks head out of window.*] You don't say so. [*Disappears.*]

Mar. [*Turning sharply.*] Yes, I *do* say so, and if you was listenin' you didn't hear nothin' more than the plain, baldheaded facts. [*Goes L. as* **Ezra** *enters from door.*]

Zach. [*Comes down and shakes hands.*] Good day, Brother Meeker. I was disappointed not to see you with your good wife at the meeting. We are doing great work, Brother Meeker, a great work. [*Going C. with Ezra.*]

Ezra. So was I, Brother Smarden. I was doin' great work, too. I 'tended to my stock, mended the light spring wagon, 'iled the harness and washed my feet.

Deacon. Better assist us in savin' this land from the liquor traffic, even if your chores are never done.

Ezra. [C.] Nor my feet washed, nuther?

Zach. [L. C.] Cleanliness is next to godliness, Brother Meeker. But we need you in this glorious work of reform.

Ezra. You don't say so. Well, that hain't the way I made my money—tendin' to other peoples' business and neglectin' my own.

Zach. Very true, Brother Meeker, but do not forget thou art thy brother's keeper.

Ezra. Not now—I was. [*Lays L. hand on* **Zach's** *shoulder.*] I kep' Bob goin' on five year, but last spring I made him git out and hustle for himself. [**Zach.** *starts to go.*] Hold on, though, mebbe brothers-in-law don't count.

Zach. Every man is our brother, as the good book says.

Ezra. [*Crossing L.*] That's what Bob banked on in my case.

Got so at last that he kinder looked to me for everything from new pants to chewin' terbacker. I stood it till he tried to borry my store teeth and then I quit.

Mar. [R. C.] I'd be ashamed, Ezra, and poor Bob enjoyin' such poor health, with dyspepsy and pain in the back. [*Sits on doorstep, angrily.*]

Ezra. Didn't have no wuss pain in the back than I did after holdin' him up five year, I reckon.

Zach. I meant that we will be held responsible for our brethren.

Ezra. Yes, when we back their note or go responsible. I went responsible for Bob and had to settle the bill.

Zach. [C.] What I mean is that we must answer for every stumbling block we put in the way of our brethren. Brother Meeker. The liquor traffic, for instance——

Ezra. [*Takes c.* **Zach.** *drops down to* R. *with* **Mar.**] Now, look a-here, Brother Smarden, you're edgin' up to Lem Davis again, hain't ye? Well, as long as liquor is made men are bound to get it if they want it. If three-qnarters of the folks in town want it, you can't make 'em quit wantin' it and gettin' it, too, by passin' laws. Contrarywise, if three-quarters of the people in town *don't* want it, dad fetch me if I can see what right they have to make the other quarter knuckle down to their idees. I don't, by gracious!

Deacon. [*Crosses* L.] But the majority have a right to rule. Ezra, and when a law is passed the minority's got to abide by it. [*Spits. Chewing all the time.*]

Ezra. [*Follows him to* L. C.] You don't say so. I think I see folks abidin' by every fool law every fool legislature ever passed. Go 'long, Seth. Suppose three-quarters of the folks in town was of a religion different from yourn, and they passed an ordinance that the other quarter had to jine their church or move out. How about that? [*Goes* R. C. *triumphantly.*]

Mar. Ezra Meeker, you allus was the biggest fool in seven counties. You can't argey. [*Rises.*] Now it just comes down to this: Be you goin' to turn that Davis out, or be you not?

Ezra. Not on your tintype. He pays his rent regular, and if I don't lease to him some one else will.

Zach. [R. C.] Then you are an enemy of the temperance cause.

Ezra. No such a thing, but I'm not payin' taxes for my health. [*Going* C.]

Zach. Those who are not for us are against us, and the good book says, "woe unto him that giveth his neighbor strong drink."

Ezra. [c. *in front of seat.*] That don't hit me—I never treat. [*Sits c. and crosses legs, swinging foot.*]

Deacon. [L.] Suppose your son Harry falls a victim to the Chicago saloonkeepers that goes about like a ragin' lion seeking what they can devour?

Ezra. Harry drink liquor? Sho, Deacon—you don't know that boy. Why, he walks nine miles every day to save ten cents car fare.

Zach. I'm afraid you are paying too much attention to the dollars, Brother Meeker. The town needs reforming, and as an instrument in the hands of Providence, I propose to reform it.

Ez. You don't say so. Say, if you'd lived here as long as I have you'd be scared to tackle it. You ask Tom Barton, our police force.

Zach. Heaven will give me strength.

Ezra. [*Rises.*] You hain't never seen Davis, have ye?

Zach. Not yet. In fact I do not propose to parley with the enemy, but to exterminate him. Well, good day to you. Good day, Sister Meeker. [*Goes up L. C. with Deacon.*]

Mar. Good day, Brother Smarden; good day, Deacon. [*As they go up.*] I hope the conference with the mayor will turn out as we wish.

Zach. Pray for us, Sister Meeker. [*Going L. U. E.*]

Mar. Indeed I will. [*Ex. Zach and Deacon L. U. E.*] Ezra Meeker, hain't you most ashamed to death to talk to a preacher that a way? Hain't you, now?

Ezra. Not a durn bit. [*Sitting c.*]

Mar. Then you'd ought to be.

Ezra. You don't say so.

Mar. Yes, I *do* say so. What's more, they'll be a judgment on you yet.

Ezra. Nobody's suein' me, and I stand in with the sheriff.

Mar. I meant a judgment from above, you old sinner. Your barn'll burn down, or your buildin's on Main street, or the whitecaps 'll git you and Lem Davis, or sumpin'—see if they don't.

Ezra. You don't say so. If the whitecaps pester with this old jay they'll find their Uncle Ezra hot company. Whitecaps? Well, I guess not.

Mar. Go on and blow, you old wind bag. Over to Clark's corners, last night, they licked old Abe Carter like sixty for sellin' liquor, and served him right, too.

Ezra. You don't say so. [*Rises. Going.*] Well, they won't Abe Carter me. When they come they'll find me watchin' for 'em. [*Aside.*] And ready to sprint at the drop of a hat. I can run like a three-year-old. [*Ex. into house.*]

Mar. That's the way it is whenever anythin' touches his pocket. When he gits his hands onto a dollar he grips it till the goddess of liberty screeches murder. But I must sound that gal about Brother Smarden. [*Calls at door.*] Elsie—oh, Elsie--here.

Elsie. [*Within.*] In a second, mother. I'm just changing my dress.

Mar. That's right, darter. Allus be careful of your, clothes. [**Elsie** *re-enters.*] Well, how do you like Brother Smarden.

Elsie. Why, mother, I -- he -- [*confused. Sits c.*]

Mar. [L. C.] Don't you try to fool your mother, Miss Innocence. I see you and him gittin' mighty confidential. Say—do you know what he told me?

Elsie. What, mother?

Mar. That of all the gals he ever heard leadin' the singin' you had the only voice that sounded like a stray note straight from paradise. How's that?

Elsie. Oh, mother!

Mar. Makes you blush, don't it? Then I told him what a right smart housekeeper you was, and how economical, makin' all your own dresses, and how much propity and money in bank your paw had, and then I kinder hinted that a revivalist without a wife didn't sorter carry so much weight——

Elsie. Mother! [*Rising.*] What must the man think of me? How could you cheapen me like that? It was cruel. Oh, I feel so mean—so mean. [*Weeps, with back to audience.*]

Mar. Well, forever and forever more! You've got him, I tell you, if you only handle him right, and you can thank your maw for it.

Elsie. I never want to see him again. Oh, mother, how could you do it? I'm so ashamed—I never was so humiliated in all my life.ᵉ [*Ex. into house, sobbing.*]

Mar. Sakes alive! I don't know what's got into the gals nowadays. I'd a-been tickled to death if *my* maw had helped me to git the feller I wanted. [*Ex. into house. Heard in house.*] How dast you. Ezra Meeker, how dast you clutter up my kitchen like that, and spill ile all over the floor that poor child scrubbed this mornin' on her bended knees. Git out of this! [*Noise of a scuffle.*]

Ezra. [*Within*] Doggone it, Mariar, quit now. I didn't do it a-purpose. [*Another scuffle and crockery crash.*] Quit, now, will ye?

Mar. [*Shouting*] I'll learn you—[*sound of beating. Whack!*

Whack!]—I'll learn you to cut up like a dog before the preacher. [*Whack! Whack!*] I'll learn you to take the wages of sin from that Lem Davis, I will. [*Whack! Whack!*] I'll learn you to be a Christian if I have to break every bone in your body doin' it. [*Door opens.* **Ezra** *is pitched or falls out. Harness thrown on top of him.*]

Ezra. Help, murder, police!

Mar. [*At door.*] That'll learn you who's boss in this house, anyhow.

Ezra. You don't say so. [*Sitting on stage.*]

Mar. Yes I do say so. Now you take them harness to the barn and then turn in and finish peelin' them pertaters. [*Goes to him and hands him dishpan with potatoes in it.*] I'll find that Pickles and lam her good; I'll learn her to break my plates, the young imp. [*Ex.* R. I. E. *calling*] Pickles! oh, Pickles!

Ezra. What a sweet angel she'll make. Ever since she got holiness, so she can't sin no more, she's like a she tomcat every time her dander's riz. Reckon I'd better take them harness to the barn or she's liable to murder me. [*Rises and looks off* R. I. E. *as* **Pickles** *begins howling within.*] She's got Pickles and she's givin' her fits. [*Sound of slapping and* **Pickles** *bawling* "Oh, don't, mam," *etc.*] I pity the cherubims when Mariar takes to runnin' the golden streets. [**Pickles** *rushes on* R. I. E. **Ezra** *holds her* R. C.] What's she been doin' to you?

Pickles. Lemme go, Pap, lemme go. She's after me with a club for breakin' them dishes.

Mar. [*Off* R. I. E.] Wait till I lay hands on you.

Pickles. Lemme go, Pap, quick. Lemme hide. I know a good place. [**Mar.** *runs on with stick.*] Don't let her hit me, Pap, please don't. [*She gets behind* **Ezra**, *who picks up harness.*]

Mar. [R. *corner.*] Let go that gal, Ezra Meeker. She needs correctin', and I'm goin' to do it. I'm responsible to the county for her raisin'.

Ezra. I'm responsible to the county for her *life*. You don't have to correct her with a club, Mariar.

Mar. Let her go, then, and I'll only spank her. [*Goes to entrance and throws club off.*

Ezra. [*Aside.*] Here's your chance, Pickles—scoot. [**Pickles** *runs.* **Mar.** *after her.* *Chase around stage.* **Ezra** *drops harness in front of* **Mar.** *who falls.*] Foot it Pickles, foot it for all you're worth. [*Ex.* **Pickles** L.]

Mar. [L. C.] If I wa'nt a Christian, I'd swear. You baldheaded old villain. [*Rises.*] Oh, oh—that fall has lamed my back. [*Limping.*] Oh, oh—it has broke my spine. [*Sits* C.]

Ezra. [R. C.] If it had only lamed your tongue, Mariar, I'd forgive it.

Mar. If you'd only broke your neck awhile ago I'd forgive you.

Ezra. You don't say so.

Mar. Wait till I lay hands on that young imp,

Ezra. You touch her again and I'll get you persecuted by the human society for cruelty to animals. [*Crosses* L.]

Mar. I'll send her back to the poor house, where you took her from.

Ezra. So do, Mariar, but you don't get no hired gal. All Pickles costs is her keep.

Mar. [*Rises.*] Ezra Meeker, I've been the head of this family nigh onto thirty year, and when I hire help you'll pay 'em. What's more, I tell you pointedly, you've got to mend your manners from this day forth.

Ezra. You don't say so. Want me to pattern on yourn, mebbe.

Mar. [C.] I'll just give you a hint that you hain't no fit father-in-law for a preacher.

Ezra. Don't want to be, nuther. Hain't got no use for preachers. As for your latest craze, Smarden, the man hain't been here two weeks yet.

Mar. Yes, but he's took holt powerful. He's took the hull town in hand.

Ezra. Looks as if he'd take anything in hand he could lay his hands *on*, and skip with it. If Elsie has gone and got stuck on him I *hain't*.

Mar. *You* don't have to marry him.

Ezra. If I did I'd be tempted to pizen him and live alone. What does Elsie say?

Mar. What does any gal say at first? What did I say when you first came cavortin' round me, Ezra Meeker?

Ezra. You just kinder reached out with both hands and hung onto me like grim death.

Mar. No such a thing. I said I wouldn't have you if you was covered with gold and di'monds. Didn't I?

Ezra. You did, Mariar, you did. Oh, if you'd only stuck to that!

Mar. More fool me I didn't. They was lots of fellers after me—John Henery Thompson, fer instance.

Ezra. Yes; he got my gal and I got hisn—worse luck. [*Goes up and sits* C.] Say, Mariar, John Henry is right welcome to you now, if he's fool enough.

Mar, [R. C.] If it wa'n't for my thirds in the propity I'd have up and got a divorce long ago.

Ezra. You don't say so!

Mar. Yes I do say so.

Ezra. You take your thirds and quit and I'll throw in the in the brindle heifer and $10 to boot. Hain't nothin' stingy about Ezra Meeker. ·

Mar. All fired anxious to git rid of me, hain't you? Well, you can't do it. [*Going to house.*] The brindle heifer and ten dollars to boot! He wants to take up with some young gal. Oh, I'm so mad I could holler. Ten dollars to boot! [*Ex. into house.*]

Ezra. Reckon I'd better find Pickles, and git her to peel them pertaters. [*Rises, goes* L. *and calls.*] Pickles, oh, Pickles!

Pickles. [*Off.*] Coo-ee—hello Dad—is she gone?

Ezra. You bet she is—gone crazy. Come here. I want ye. [*Beckoning her. Goes* R.]

Pickles. [*Enters* L. 2 E.] Say, did she skull drag you? Let's see. [*Lifts his hat.*] Gee! I expected she'd have you plucked cleaner'n a geese.

Ezra. [R. C.] Naw—she's quit draggin' my hair out by the roots ever since she got religion—only takes a club to me now. I wisht she'd started that long ago—I'd a had more hair.

Pickles. Poor old Dad.

Ezra. Say, don't you ever let her hear ye call me Dad. It's like shakin' a red rag at a bull.

Pickles. Why so?

Ezra. 'Cause I came pretty nigh bein' your father once.

Pickles. Go 'long! Then why didn't you?

Ezra. 'Cause your mother wouldn't have me. Then I was durn fool enough to turn round and marry Mariar Martin for spite. They hain't nobody to blame only me—and Mariar, Mariar mostly. Gee, how she did chase me up. Oh, well—come along—bring them 'taters behind the house and we'll peel 'em on shares. [*Ex. with* **Pick.** R. I. E. **Jaggsy** *enters* L. U. E *half drunk, comes down to well and draws cup of water. Raises it to his lips two or three times and puts it down disgusted.*]

Jaggsy. No—I can't go it. My stomach's too delicate. Wonder where Gusta Ann is? She might have a nickel or two for her poor old father. [*Looks off* R. I. E.] Why, there she is as large as life. [*Calls softly.*] Gusta—Gusta—Gusta Ann. Hears me and don't reconize her own christened name. [*Calls*] Oh, Pickles. [*Beckons.*]

Pickles. [*Off.*] Hello, Pop. What you want?

Jag. Want to see you special. [*Goes* C.]

Pickles. [*Enters* R. I. E.] Well, if you ain't a sight. Drinkin, again, *hain't* ye?

Jag. Not a drop. I've reformed. Went to the temperance rally to-day and got caught in the wave. [*Sings*] "I've been redeemed—I've been redeemed—"

Pickles. [R. C.] Say, Pop, would you just as lief sing as make that noise? Now, do you mean to say you've swore off again?

Jag. That's what. I've turned over a new leaf.

Pickles. Best sit on it and keep it turned this trip, Pop. You've signed the pledge eight times already. Every time you backslided you told a lie, and Mam Meeker she 'lows we git a hundred years in the bad place for every whopper, so you'll have eight hundred years to burn. [*Crosses* L.]

Jag. Gosh—ain't it awful.

Pickles. Mam didn't tell me how long they give you for gettin' full, but I reckon they'll cook you up pretty good for that, too. Your only chance is to jine the church, Pop.

Jag. I'll do it, Gusta Ann, the minute I can lay my hands on some good clothes. [*Sits* C.]

Pickles. Goody, Pop, goody! But, say, when you git to layin' hands on them clothes be right careful the feller 'at owns 'em ain't lookin'—won't ye now?

Jag. Gusta Ann, don't you go to trifle with the feelin's of a reformed man. I've quit swipin'.

Pickles. Ah, git out. You're joshin' me.

Jag. Dead earnest. Moreover, I've started workin'.

Pickles. Oh, come off.

Jag. Fact. Postmaster Soper hired me to hustle up here with these letters for Elsie Meeker. He's goin' to gimme a dime. How's that?

Pickles. Splendid, Pop—splendid. [*Crossing* R.] Say, that's the first lick of work you've done in goin' on four year, ain't it?

Jag. That's what. Oh, I've reformed, I tell ye. [*Rises, goes* R. *to her.*] Say, Gusta Ann, let me take a dime and I'll give it to you when the Deacon pays me.

Pickles. What you want it for?

Jag. I want to git a bath.

Pickles. Nixy, Pop, nixy. You wantin' a bath is just spreadin' it on a little too thick. Besides, I ain't had a dime since the one Harry Meeker gimme Fourth of July, which you borryed and blew in at Lem Davis's.

Jag. I'm goin' to pay you that dime on the installment plan, Pickles, [*going* C.] a cent a month. In ten months you'll have your money back.

Pickles. [*Following him* c.] Say, you *are* gittin' honest—hain't ye?

Jag. You bet I am. Where's Elsie?

Pickles. Gimme the letters—I'll take 'em to her.

Jag. Can't be did. I'm a special delivery.

Pickles. All right, Pop. [*Goes* R.] Only don't let Dad Meeker see ye or he'll sick the dog onto ye. [*Ex. into house.*]

Jag. That reform gag fetched her. I'm on the right track. The latest fad is reform, and I'll work it.

Elsie. [*Entering from house.*] You have letters for me, Mr. Thompson?

Jag. [c.] Yes'm, two of 'em. [*Hands letters.*] The special delivery one is all paid for by the stamp.

Elsie. [c.] Oh, is there postage due on the other?

Jag. Well, no—not postage ezackly—but I thought the walk might be worth somethin'. They hain't no claim, Miss Meeker. It's all owin' to whether you think it's worth a nickel.

Elsie. [*Laughing.*] To be sure it is. Why, this is from Harry and this from Cousin Lou. [*Coming down.*]

Jag. Oh, me and the postmaster reckoned they wa'n't no *love* letters. We knew Harry's writin', and we both 'lowed the other was a female letter. Well, I'll be off. [*Pause. Fill in business here.*] I said I must be goin' now.

Elsie. Oh, excuse me--the nickel. I forgot. [*Gives money.*]

Jag. Thanks. [*Aside.*] Beer! [*Ex. L. U. E. on a dead run.*]

Elsie. [*Laughing.*] Poor Jaggsy. I suppose I shouldn't laugh, but I can't help it. [*Laughs. Sits* c.]

Will. [*Enters* L. 2 E.] May I laugh, too. [*Law book in hand.*]

Elsie. Why, Will—how you startled me!

Will. [L. c.] I didn't mean to do that—

Elsie. Oh, there's no harm done. [*Makes room and he sits beside her.*] How do you get along with your law?

Will. It's pretty hard work to labor all day and then read for a profession at odd times and at night.

Elsie. You are ambitious, Will, and I believe you'll succeed.

Will. Thanks. I *am* ambitious, Miss Elsie. I have set myself to reach a goal so distant that it almost frightens me to think of it. But whatever is worth winning is worth working and waiting for.

Elsie. How soon do you expect to go to Chicago?

Will. As soon as I have saved two hundred dollars more.

Elsie. You deserve to succeed, and I only wish I could help you.

Will. You *can* help me—you do.

Elsie. I do? How?

Will. [*Rises.*] I dare not explain now. Remember that I have set myself to reach a goal so distant that I sometimes grow faint-hearted when I try to measure the path I have to climb.

Elsie. [*Rising.*] Why, Will, you are talking in riddles. What has all that got to do with my helping you?

Will. You first inspired me to struggle on, and opened up a new path to my ambition.

Elsie. [R. C. *Looking down at ground.*] I was interested in you, of course.

Will. [*Close to her.*] Where others laughed, you appreciated the uphill task I had undertaken, and encouraged me. Can't you see the inevitable result? I learned to love you—to almost worship you as the one good angel—the one true woman in my life.

Elsie. Why, Will—Mr. Goodall—I never suspected this. Please don't think I have intentionally led you to believe I cared for you, because—because——

Will. Don't, Elsie—don't say there is no hope for me.

Elsie. Mr. Goodall—I—

Will. [*Turns.*] Not Mr. Goodall, Elsie—say Will, as you always have, and the sentence of death to all my hopes will seem less cruel from your lips.

Elsie. [*Goes up to him.*] Truly, Will, I respect and sympathize with you. Even more, I admire you for your courage and ambition, but I never even thought of you as a lover.

Will. May I ask just one rude question?

Elsie. If it is not too rude.

Will. You shall judge. Is there anybody else?

Elsie. [*Getting away from him.*] That is rather personal. You mean do I love another man?

Will. Exactly.

Elsie. Well, I do.

Will. Then it is all over with me. [*Goes L.*] The law may go to pot. [*Flings book L.*]

Elsie. [C.] Why, Will Goodall, I thought you had more grit than that.

Will. Who is he? I beg your pardon, I have no right to ask. [*Comes down.*]

Elsie. It was dreadfully rude, but I'll answer. [*Coming down.*] I'll also confess that I've been in love with him ever since we were children. We were raised together, and I think him the handsomest, the most brilliant, the gentlest, the bravest and the kindest man I ever knew. Oh, I just think the world of him! [*Down R. C.*]

Will. [L. C.] Happy fellow. I'd give ten years of my life to hear you say that of me. Won't you tell me his name?

Elsie. I don't think I should. You men do such awful things when jealousy inspires you.

Will. [*Goes close to her.*] You don't know me, Elsie. I love you so truly that should the chance ever come I will be this man's friend, if it takes my last dollar or even my life.

Elsie. Will, you are a good fellow, and I am going to tell you his name, no matter what happens. He is—he is—

Will. Well?

Elsie. [*Gets away from him.*] My brother Harry. [*Runs into house, laughing.*]

Will. [*Crossing L.*] I guess the law hadn't better got to pot just yet. [*Picks up book and ex. L. 2 E.*]

Elsie. [*Re-enters, watching him off.*] Who'd ever have thought of Will Goodall being in love with me? He's ever so much nicer than Mr. Smarden, too—ugh! That man's very name gives me the creepies. [*Goes c. and sits.*] Now, which shall I open first? Cousin Lou's—I'll save up the good things till the last. [*Opens letter and reads.*]

"My Dear Elsie:—I don't want you to think mean of me, because what I am doing is my duty and for his good." Now, who on earth is *he?* That's just like Lou—she always gets everything all mixed up. "I thought better to write you than Uncle Ezra or Aunt Maria, because you always have so much influence with him." Well, who is *him?* "Mrs. Brown says he has been drinking hard and staying out nights till all hours, and her boarders are all quiet folks, and she thinks he has something on his mind and it drives him to drink, and the other boarders won't stand it much longer." Well, isn't that lucid? "So I think you had better have him home for a time and get him to tell his troubles and make him swear off liquor. So no more at present from Lou." Why—she means—oh, nonsense--she can't mean Harry. Our Harry drink? Impossible! [*Nervously opens the other letter.*] Perhaps this will explain. [*Reads.*] "My Dear Sister:—You will no doubt be surprised when I tell you that I am in an awful fix. I know you will despise me. I got in with a fast lot of fellows, Sis, and between drinking and the races I have dropped $200 more than I have earned, and I can't keep the shortage hidden beyond the first of the month. I am coming home to see what I can do with father or Davis, but had to write and tell you first. Don't hate me, Sis. I have been weak and wicked, but if I get out of this I will never taste liquor again as long as I live. Harry."

My brother a defaulter—a thief! Oh, Harry, Harry, how could you do it, how could you? [*Weeps.* **Will** *re-enters.*]

Will. [L. C. *Aside.*] This is my fault. I was too abrupt and frightened her. [*Aloud.*] Don't cry, Elsie. It shames me to see you in tears and to know that my own lack of self-control has caused them. Come, dry your eyes—a hired man isn't worth crying over, anyway.

Elsie. It isn't your fault, Will. It isn't you who have broken my heart, but the one I loved and had such faith in. Oh, Harry, Harry!

Will. What, your brother in trouble? Won't you tell me all about it and let me help him?

Elsie. No. No, Will—I couldn't tell you; you couldn't help him. He doesn't deserve help—he has been wicked, wicked.

Will. Don't say that—you don't know how strong his temptation may have been. Come, tell me what the trouble is.

Elsie. I couldn't tell you this—I couldn't bear even to let father or mother know—then how could I expose his degradation to a stranger?

Will. [*Sitting beside her.*] Believe me, two heads are better than one, so let me help you—let me help him.

Elsie. I must bear this sorrow alone.

Will. As you wish, but if there is anything I can do, don't hesitate to let me know. Nothing could give me so much pleasure as to make you happy.

Elsie. You are too good, too kind to me, Will. I don't deserve it.

Will. It is not your fault that I fell in love with you, Elsie, but my misfortune. And yet, even if I could control my fate and had the past few months to live over again, I would still love you.

Elsie. I am sorry, Will—sorry, sorry—but I can give you no encouragement.

Will. I know it. That is why I am going to Chicago to-morrow night.

Elsie. Oh, Will, I am driving you away.

Will. It will be better for both of us. [*Rising.*] I am going to enter the law school and trust to hard work to carry me through.

Elsie. [*Rises*] You are brave, Will—and I shall pray for your [*gives her hand*] success. There—we are true friends now—God bless you.

Will. [*Conducts her to house.*] God bless you, dear. [*Ex.* **Elsie** *into house.*] Oh, if I only had the right to take her to my heart and comfort her. [*Crossing to c.*] I wonder what that boy has done? Something serious, I expect. I'll have to hunt him up as soon as I get to the city. [**Lem Davis** *enters hurriedly* L. U. E. *Comes down* C.]

Lem. Hello, young feller, where's your boss?

Will. [C] If you mean Mr. Meeker, he's about the place, somewhere.

Lem. [R. C.] That's just who I do mean. Git a slide on you now and tell him I want him. I'm Lem Davis, see?

Will. I know who you are. The other night I helped to carry Jaggsy Thompson home dead drunk after you threw him into the street and cut a gash in his head against the curbing.

Lem. Suppose I did? What business is it of yours, anyway?

Will. I'd mighty soon make it my business if I were mayor of this town.

Lem. Is *that* so? Well, you just keep your hand on your mouth till you *are* mayor, and then you can commence shootin' it off. See? Now git a hump on ye and tell old man Meeker I want him. [*Crosses* L.]

Will. If you want Mr. Meeker you'd better go and look for him. [*Goes a little up* C.]

Lem. Huh! Suppose you're another of the temperance push that thinks its runnin' this town. Well, we've got the mayor and all kinds of money to buy votes next election. You can't down the saloon in this berg. See?

Will. Give it rope enough, and by its own arrogant corruption the saloon will down itself. It will force into active opposition every citizen with a spark of decency, manhood or patriotism in him.

Lem. Oh, rats!

Will. [C.] Thousands of men who are neither prohibitionists nor total abstainers are arraying themselves against it because they see that it is the saloon that leads our boys astray, blights the lives of our young men, breaks up happy homes and brings down grey hairs in shame and sorrow to the grave. It makes widows weep and orphans mourn. It condemns women and children to suffer the pangs of hunger and shiver with bitter cold. It dominates and corrupts our politics, defies our laws and makes thieves of honest men. It is the central plague spot from which radiates every dread disease that afflicts the body politic; beginning with debauchery and ending with murder, suicide and death. They see that the saloon, which by some of its apologists has been called the poor man's club, is, in fact, the poor man's pitfall. It makes the rich richer and the poor poorer by filching from the pockets of those who can least afford it millions of hard-earned dollars every year. It is the devil's workshop, impurity's chief agent and the headquarters of crime and criminals.

Lem. Say, you're too smart. What you want is a good slap on the mouth.

Will. No, I don't—and you don't want to give it to me, either.

Lem. Just you lip me a little more and I'll give you a push in the face that'll make you see stars.

Will. Don't try to bulldoze me. I know you thoroughly—you and your kind—one-half fawning cringe to the man who has money to spend, and the other half impudent bully to the man you think you may safely browbeat.

Lem. Say, you're lookin' for fight—you'll get it. [*Strikes at* **Will,** *who avoids the blow and counters, landing on the chest.* **Lem** *spins around a couple of times and falls in a heap just as* **Ezra** *enters.* R. I. E. **Will** *goes* L.]

Ezra. [*At entrance.*] You don't say so! Time! Why, what you tryin' to do, Lem? Tired of standin' up? Or are you just measurin' yourself for a new grave?

Lem. [C. *Rising.*] I'll show him. [**Ezra** *holds him.*] Let me go—let me go, I tell ye. I'll do that mug if I never do another thing.

Ezra. Hold on, Lem—hold on now. What's all the row about, anyhow?

Lem. His temperance joblots there first insults me about my business and then soaks me when my back is turned for cracking back at him.

Ezra. [R. C.] What have you got to say to this, Bill?

Will. [L. *corner.*] That he lies. I only stopped him in self-defense.

Ezra. There's no harm done, anyway, so you go round to the shed, Bill, and chop some wood for the old woman to get dinner with. [*Crosses* L.]

Lem. [*As* **Will** *crosses* R.] Say, young feller, the next time you see me comin' you'd best have on your runnin' shoes. See? [*Spits.*]

Will. [*Stops at entrance.*] Yelping curs don't often bite. [*Ex.* R. I. E.]

Lem. Say, Ezra, who is that duck? [*Crossing to* **Ezra.**]

Ezra. Bill Goodall. Been with me four months, and this is the first time I ever saw his rough side.

Lem. I'll not forget *him.* Well, what do you suppose brings me here?

Ezra. [*Looks around cautiously.*] To pay me my share of the business, I suppose.

Lem. Well, I didn't. It's about this here temperance epidemic. This crazy Smarden, Soper and the rest of the executive committee have the mayor's ear.

Ezra. You don't say so? Did he give it to 'em or only loan it?

Lem. They're holdin' a confab at the town hall right now, and Tom Barton has been called before 'em.

Ezra. You don't say so.

Lem. Well, I *do* say so, and at the meetin' this mornin' Smarden said our saloon had to go if they had to start it with dynamite. I'm afraid they'll blow me up.

Ezra. They won't blow nothin' only their bazoo. [*Crosses to c. and sits.*] . They wanted me to throw you out, but I told 'em nixy.

Lem. Then you don't think they'll do no dynamitin' or whitecappin'?

Ezra. Not a bit of it. This is only one of them spazzums folks gits onto 'em every once in so often. This temperance spouter has 'em all hypnotized, but he'll soon wear out.

Lem. I haven't saw that skate yet. [*Sits beside* **Ezra.**]

Ezra. You shouldn't say "I haven't saw," Lem; that hain't grammar. You should say "I haven't sawn." But you'll see him he's bound to stop in and wrastle with you. He tackled me this mornin'. Say, wouldn't the drys have a fit if they knew we were pardners?

Lem. Your wife wouldn't do a thing to you, would she? Say, Ezra, there's mighty strong talk of whitecappin' me, and if they knew we was pardners, you'd git it sure. [*Rises.*]

Ezra. Well, they won't know, if you don't tell 'em. [*Rises.*]

Tom. [*Entering L. U. E.*] Howdy, fellers—heard the news? [*Crosses to c. and comes down.*]

Ezra. No—what's the row?

Tom. [*Down c.*] The mayor's done the flop act over to the drys.

Ezra. You don't say so! [R. C. **Lem.** *is* L. C.]

Tom. He's give me orders to close out Lem, here, and stick every blind pig in town, besides runnin' out the gamblers.

Ezra. You don't say so.

Tom. That's what I *said* and what *he* said, too. [*To Lem.*] Mayor Spraddlin says you've got to close up instanter, which means right off, to once, and no monkeyin'.

Ezra. You d——

Tom. I *do* say so.

Lem. [L. C.] All right. I'll close.

Ezra. Front door and back?

Tom. Front door and back.

Ezra. Old Spraddlin's a condemned eejit—that's what he is. How does he s'pose the boys is goin' to git a drink?

Tom. They'll have to tackle the boot leg, I reckon.

Lem. Oh, I've got things all fixed. They can't freeze me out. Here, Tom. [*Gives note.*]

Tom. What's this for?

Lem. Cigars.

Tom. A ten spot! Thanks. [*Puts money in pocket.*]

Lem. And don't you go to the Dutchman's for your smokes. You keep away from there, and when you see any of the good boys, tell 'em to slip down the Dutchman's back stairs into the basement and they're liable to find me entertainin' the push with pop and sich. [*Goes a little up L.*] Do you catch on?

Tom. Well, do I? [*Goes up.*]

Zach. [*Enters L. U. E.*] What are you doing here Barton? [*Up C. He comes down.* Maria, Elsie *and* Will *re-enter.* Mar. *and* Elsie *stand at door.* Will *stays at R. I. E.*]

Tom. Mayor Spraddlin' told me to close up Lem Davis, and as he wasn't at the saloon, I followed him here to give him fair warnin'.

Zach. [*Recognizes* Lem *and starts.*] It was your duty to arrest all you found in the groggery and run the liquor into the gutter.

Mar. Right, Brother Smarden, right. So the mayor is on our side at last! Praise the Lord!

Zach. [c.] Amen to that, Sister Meeker. The glorious wave of reform has started to roll, and we'll never let it stop until this town is washed clean from every vice and villainy. [R. C.]

Ezra. [*Sitting* c.] You don't say so. See here, Smarden, 'pears to me you're settin' up to be mayor, city council, sheriff, chief of police, judge, jury, and the hull thing. [*Drops down to L. corner.*]

Zach. [R. C.] It is my mission to purge this community of all that is corrupt. [Pickles *enters* R. I. E. Tom *is* L. C.]

Lem. Then you'd better start in with yourself. You are Zachariah Smarden, are ye? Well, before you shaved them whiskers, when I was a guard at Fort Madison penitentiary, you went by the name of Jim Cooke, otherwise Jim the Penman, and you was doin' a three-years' stretch for forgery. [*Points at him. All start in surprise.* Zach. *appears terrified.*]

Picture. Quick curtain.

ACT II.

[Kitchen at Meeker's. Plain chamber in 3d grooves. Boxed scene. Doors R. 3 E. and L. 2 E. and R. in flat. Hat rack on flat near door. Window L. in flat. Kitchen dresser R. against scene. Table up stage C. with ironing board extending from it to chair L. Clothes horse with ironing on it, clothes basket, rough dry clothes, etc. Two chairs R. Rocker L. C. At rise **Maria** and **Pickles** ironing. **Ezra** and **Elsie** down R. playing checkers at small table. **Will** and **Harry** L. packing valise.]

Ezra. [L. of table. Moving piece.] I'm into kingdom come. Put a crown on that one, Elsie. [They play throughout scene.]

Mar. [Up C.] Ezra Meeker, if you'd on'y read your Bible a little more and play them sinful games a little less, mebbe you would get into kingdome come sure 'nuff.

Ezra. I hain't a-hankerin' for kingdom come—not jest this minute, Mariar. I've kinder got used to bein' on earth.

Mar. And mebbe it 'ud be give to you to see a light and quit sendin' immortal souls to the bad place by selling 'em liquor.

Ezra You don't say so.

Mar. [Slamming down iron.] Yes, I do say so. I hold it ain't nothin' more nor less than bein' pardners with Lem Davis when you rent to him, and they'll be a judgment onto ye yet—you'll see.

Ezra. You don't say so.

Mar. See here, Ezra Meeker, you've a'most pestered me to death ever since you got aholt of that slang, "You don't say so." Now you quit it or I'll throw somepin' at you as sure's you're a foot high.

Ezra. You don't say so.

Mar. [Throwing flat iron.] Yes I do say so.

Ezra. It's a good thing your strenth wa'n't as good's your will, or you'd a flattened me out sure. They hain't no call to git so all-fired ironical.

Mar. [*Coming down* c.] Served you right if I'd abroke your head or mashed your bunions.

Ezra. A bunion or a pertater's about the only thing you *can* mash, Mariar.

Mar. Hain't heard tell of any weemin' goin' to the asylum on your account, Ezra.

Ezra. If you don't quit your naggin' they'll be one poor man go there on your account. You're just about the henpeckinest old henpecker that ever a henpecked man got henpecked by— them's your specifications.

Mar. You're a fool, that's what you are. [*Goes up, after picking up iron.*]

Ezra. Then there's a pair of us, so it's a stand-off. [*Continues game with* **Elsie.** **Mar.** *irons viciously.* **Pickles** *busy all the time.*]

Will. [L. *Strapping valise.*] Thanks—that fixes it. I'm sorry I won't see more of you, but I must go tonight.

Har. [L. C.] I'd hate to take that night's ride and sit up.

Will. I've got to do it to keep down expenses. [*Both sit.*] By the way, there is something I've been trying to say to you all evening, but I don't know how to begin. It might seem impertinent in a stranger.

Har. Well, as I don't like impertinence, perhaps you'd better not begin at all.

Will. And yet I take a lot of interest in you.

Har. Thanks—that's *so* good of you.

Will. Don't get sarcastic, there's a good fellow. This matter is more important to you than to me.

Har. What are you driving at?

Will. After your sister read your letter the day before yesterday, she nearly cried her eyes out.

Har. What has that got to do with you?

Will. I am a good deal interested in her, also.

Har. Yes—I've noticed that—I admire your nerve.

Will. See here, don't act like a young jackass. Don't you see that I want to befriend you?

Har. I didn't ask you for friendship. I can handle my own business, thank you.

Will. I don't believe you can. Elsie told me you were in a scrape.

Har. [*Angrily raising voice.*] So she had to blab, eh? [*Rises.*]

Ezra. [*Looks up from game.*] Some gal bein' tellin' on ye, Harry? You might 'a' expected that, for no female woman can keep a secret any more'n your maw can keep her temper. Who's the gal?

Har. Oh, its nothing, father. I was annoyed for a moment, that's all.

Will. Control yourself—sit down again [**Will** *sits*]—I am bound to finish, now that I have begun. Elsie refused to tell me the nature of your trouble, but judging from your sudden visit home and the suppressed excitement you show, you are not out of it yet. Won't you tell me all about it and let me help you?

Har. See here, Mr. Goodall, your taking an interest in Sis is all right. If she and the folks like it I have nothing to say. But when that interest extends to me, I have. I'm of age, and don't want anybody prying into my affairs.

Will. Excuse me. I'm sorry I spoke. [*Rises.*]

Har. You're not mad, I hope?

Will. Oh, no—but I'm sorry you should think that vulgar curiosity was my motive.

Har. Sit down again—come, sit down, Bill. I didn't mean to act so ugly about it. I see now that you are talking to me on account of Sis.

Will. [*Sits down.*] You've guessed it.

Har. What is there between you?

Will. Nothing.

Har. Now I'm sorry I spoke.

Will. There is nothing but friendship between us—not even an understanding.

Har. Say, there's one thing I like about you—you look straight at a man, and I don't believe you'd go back on a friend.

Will. Never.

Har. Well, don't let on you know, even to Sis, and I'll tell you what the trouble is.

Will. I promise.

Har. I'm in an awful hole. I am short in my cash nearly two hundred dollars, and if I don't raise the money by the first of the month I'll be found out.

Will. That's bad. Your time is short—as well as your cash.

Har. Just so; but I'm pretty sure to get enough from the old man if I can catch him in the right humor. If not, I think Davis will lend it to me.

Will. I'd hate to be under an obligation to him.

Har. Same here, but he's my last chance.

Will. Suppose he won't lend it to you?

Har. I might as well jump into the river at once. I am

bonded with a guarantee company that makes a feature of presecuting every defaulter.

Will. It's a bad scrape. That would ruin you just as you are starting in life, and break Elsie's heart. I'll tell you what—if everything else fails, come to me and I'll help you through.

Har. [*Rises.*] You help me through?

Will. [*Rises.*] Yes, I. I have a little money that, as a last resource, I can draw on.

Har. Bill, you are a thundering good fellow, and you must be awfully in love with Sis to do this for me. [*Shakes hands.*]

Will. Put it down to Elsie. Now, boy [*lays hand on his shoulder*], I don't want to preach, but for heaven's sake, for Elsie's sake, let this be a˙ lesson to you.

Har. If it hadn't been for the saloon and the race track it never would have happened, Bill. I give you my word I'll never handle a card, bet on a horse or touch another drop of liquor as long as I live.

Will. [*Shaking hands.*] Stick to that, my boy—stick to it for your sister's sake. You don't know what an awful blow it would be to her if you should go to the bad. I never saw a girl so completely wrapped up in a brother.

Har. She's a dear, good girl, Bill, and the man who gets her will be in big luck.

Will. I'll break the tenth commandment when she marries.

Har. Oh no, you won't; for a man can't covet what's his own.

Will. There isn't much chance of that, I'm afraid.

Mar. [*c. Ironing.*] Pickles says they's a heap of whitecap talk uptown, Ezra.

Ezra. You don't say so.

Pickles. [*In front of clothes horse 1.. c.*] Sure. The saloon crowd is telling it that they is a gang made up to whip the dickens outen the leadin' wets; and the drys, they are goin' round blowin' about judgments and things that's goin˙ to happen soon.

Ezra. [*Rises and goes c.*] You don't say so. Where'd you hear all this, Pickles?

Pick. [*Coming down c.*] Pop told me. He's been doin' errants for Deacon Soper ever since he reformed, and the Deacon he up and told him this afternoon that they'd tired *prayin'* liquor out of town, and it didn't work, so now they was goin' to try *whippin'* it out. Then he sorter invited Pop to jine the Heroes of Temperance and Pop, he agreed until the Deacon told him to call round tonight for his blacksnake whip and git ready for business.

Ezra. What did your Pop do then?

Pick. Took to the woods. I see him when he was makin' a break for tall timber. [*Goes a little* L. *laughing.* **Ezra** *laughs.*]

Mar. [*Comes down* c. *with iron in hand.*] Well, it's time. They've let the other crowd trample onto 'em long enough. Temperance folks is gittin' some spunk into 'em at last.

Ezra. [R. C.] Some temperance folks 'll be gittin' a few holes into 'em, or gittin' into the penitentiary, fust thing they know.

Mar. [C.] They's got to be martyrs to every cause. Look at the early Christians. Didn't Julius Cæsar and George the Third chase 'em into a theater and feed 'em to the wild beasts? That's why Christians has been down on the theater ever since. [*Crosses and sits* L. *of table. Fans herself with apron.*]

Ezra. [R. C.] I wish I had your edication, Mariar. I'd know more about the early Christians than I do; but, see here, do you hold with this here whitecap business? [*Sits* R. *of table.*]

Mar. I hold with anythin' that'll put down lawbreakers.

Ezra. [*Talking over his shoulder.*] Then you don't reckon it lawbreakin' to drag a man outen his bed and lick seven kinds of tar outen him, hey?

Mar. Not if it's done in a Christian spirit, it ain't. Oh, I just wisht I was a man!

Ezra. [*Turns squarely round on his chair.*] I wish to the Lord you was, Mariar, afore I ever see you. Say, who writ that letter I got this afternoon?

Mar. I don't know nothin' about your letter. [*Goes up stage.*]

Ezra. Then how did it git onto the kitchen table? It's addressed to me, and it hain't got no stamp on nor nuthin'.

Mar. You'd best go and ast them as put it there. [*Ironing.*]

Ezra. I'm astin' you.

Mar. Oh, go and find out.

Ezra. It'll be a cold day for somebody when I *do* find out.

Mar. And you'll have a hot time doin' it.

Ezra. You don't say so. [*Makes move in game.*] Ha, ha, ha! [*To* Elsie.] I've got you cornered now. Ha, ha, ha! [Elsie *rises.*]

Mar. [*Mocks him.*] You don't say so. Ha, ha, ha! [*Throws flatiron.*]

Ezra. [*Jumps.*] Look a-here, Mariar, ef you must have exercise you'd best light the lantern and go out and heave rocks at the barn.

Mar. [*Picking up iron.*] You never *could* argey without gettin' mad. That's why I despise talkin' to ye. Pickles, git me a hot iron.

Pickles. Yes, ma'am. [*Ex.* R.].

Ezra. [*Goes up to* **Mar.**] You claim you don't know nothin' about this? [*Shows letter.*]

Mar. You can't prove anythin' by me. [*Looks off* R. *door.*] There's that young one playin' with the fire again. Pickles, you young limb of satan, what do you mean by that? [*Ex.* R. D.]

Har. What is the letter about, father? [*Sound of slapping.* Pickles *bawls off.*]

Ezra. Whitecaps. I hain't got my glasses, but you can read it. Read it out loud. [*Comes down* L. *Hands letter.*]

Har. "Ezra Meeker—You are warned to turn Lem Davis out of your building immediately, because he is using the premises for an unlawful purpose. If you do not give some assurance that you intend to do your duty as a good citizen in this matter before evening you may expect an early visit from   WHITECAPS."

Elsie. Oh, father, what did you do?

Ezra. [L. C.] Loaded both bar'ls of the shot gun.

Will. They haven't come yet, at all events. [*Re-enter* **Mar.**]

Ezra. You bet they hain't, the cowardly yaller dogs; they don't dast to come. They think they can scare me. '

Mar. [*Up* C.] Don't you be too sure about that, Ezra Meeker. Old Abe Carter, over to Clark's Corners, hain't been out of bed since, they tell me.

Ezra. They'll know they hain't monkeyin' with old Abe Carter if they ever tackle their Uncle Ezra. Old man Carter never fit into the war four year. *I did.* Oh, Bill, did you remember to git that dynamite?

Will. Yes. I put it under the loose ˍboard, by the manger, where you told me.

Ezra. How much was it? [**Har.** *drops down to* L. *corner.*]

Will. [L. C.] Fifty cents.

Ezra. I'll settle that when I pay you up, bime-bye. I wisht you'd make up your mind to stop over to-morrow and help me blow out them stumps. I'm skeered to handle the pesky stuff. [*Crosses* R.]

Will. I can't. I'm all packed up and my trunk is over at the depot. I have no working clothes in this valise.

Ezra. [*Sits in rocker* R. C.] Oh, I'll find you an old pair of pants an' a shirt. Come, now, say you'll stop over and I'll give you a dollar fifty for your day. That'll help pay your fare to Chicago.

Elsie. [*Crosses* L. *Aside to him.*] Please, Will, stay. I may need your help for Harry.

Will. [*Aside to* **Elsie.**] For your sake—anything. [**Elsie** *goes* *to* **Harry,** L. *corner.*] Very well—I'll stay and help you out. I might need a good turn myself, some time.

Ezra. That's the talk. Say, if them whitecaps come round tonight they'll be a circus. Eh, Bill?

Will. I expect there will. Mind you, I'm against the saloon, but I am equally against mob rule.

Mar. [*Coming down* C.] Brother Smarden says we've got to rule the saloon or let the saloon rule us, and it's gotten such a holt on us that it 'll take a revolution to make it let go. He 'lows that saloon rule is wus'n British rule, and we don't ever notice no one regrettin' that we revoluted agin' King George. That's what Brother Smarden says.

Ezra. You don't say so. Brother Smarden had better clear himself of the charges Lem Davis makes agin' him before he sets up to preach or teach decent folks their dooty.

Mar. Sho! Who'd believe Lem Davis—a saloonkeeper?

Ezra. Me for one. I've did business with Lem for goin' on four year, and I hain't found him out in a lie or a dishonest action yet, if he *is* a saloonkeeper. [**Will, Harry** *and* **Elsie** *group* L. *as if talking.*]

Mar. Well, he's lied this time, and Brother Smarden's letters of recommend shows it.

Ezra. Oh, have it your own way, Mariar—you most generally do. Smarden's an angel, that's what Smarden is. He'd be a bird only he hain't got wings. [**Maria** *goes up and irons.*] I hear that you folks up to the church is thinkin' of givin' him a call as soon as you succeed in starvin' the present pasture out.

Mar. The Rev. Balmer's as good a man as ever lived, but he's too old-fashioned and hain't got no drawin' powers, so the congregation's dwindlin' fast, and we need a change in the pulpit. He hain't been pop'lar for a long time now.

Ezra. No—hain't been pop'lar ever since he got married to Martha Strong. He pleased Marm Strong and made a mortial enemy of every other mother in the hull caboodle that had daughters, to say nothin' of the marryin' widders. Pickles, light the lantern and bring it here. [*Ex.* **Pickles** R.]

Mar. Well, I never could make out what he seen in that stuck up Strong girl.

Ezra. Mebbe it was her strenth.

Mar. Now, Pickles hurry up. I want you to help me put the ironin' away. [*Buss. of carrying off the washing and ironing board, all except what hangs on the clothes horse,* R. *door.*] As soon as I'm through, Elsie, we'll run over to Deacon Soper's **for a** minute. Would you like to go, Harry?

Har. No, mother, I'm tired after my trip; and, besides, I want to talk to father a bit. [**Pickles** *re-enters with lighted lantern.* **Maria** *ex.* R. *with clothes basket.*]

Ezra. [*Goes up* R. *Taking lantern.*] All right, sonny, I'll be back in a few minutes. Oh, Bill, come out as far as the barn. [*Bill goes up to him. Aside.*] I want to fix up a plan in case them whitecaps does show up. [*Opens door in flat.*] Phew! Say, Bill, do you smell anything?

Bill. Whew! I should say I did. There's a skunk around here, some place.

Ezra. After them chickens, by gracious. Come on, Bill. [*Ex. with* **Bill** D. 1. F., *leaving it open.*]

Mar. [*Re-entering* R.] Whew! Land of Goshen! Shut that door, Pickles; shut it quick or we'll all be smothered alive. [*Sees to closing door, and ex.* R. *with* **Pickles.**]

Elsie. [C.] Have you made up your mind to tell father, Harry?

Har. [L.] Not till I've tried everything else. Oh, sister, I'm so ashamed and penitent!

Elsie. How do you propose to get the money from him?

Har. [*Going to her.*] I'll tell him I know of a good investment for two hundred dollars that will pay him two per cent a month for seven months. It will only leave me six dollars a week, but I can live on that.

Elsie. But would it be honest?

Har. Of course. It is big interest, and you know how he loves a dollar. He'll jump at the chance.

Elsie. You had better confess everything and start anew. Concealment is sure to make more trouble, and, besides, if he gave you the money, and you should lose your position——.

Har. Oh, pshaw! You girls don't understand business. [*Crosses* R.] We've got to take *some* risks. I have Davis to fall back on, and if he fails Bill Goodall has promised to help me.

Elsie. Will Goodall! Then you have told him?

Har. While you were playing checkers. He was so kind that I couldn't help it. I say, Sis, he's awfully fond of you. [**Will** *re-enters.*]

Elsie. Hush—here he is. [*Goes* L.]

Mar. [*At* R. *door.*] Elsie Meeker, where on earth is your nose? Go and close them winders in your paw's room, for goodness sake. That critter's just smellin' the hull house up. [*Ex.* R. *door.* **Elsie** *ex.* L. *door. Window heard to slam. She re-enters at once.*]

Har. [R.] Did you kill it?

Will. [*Down* C.] No. I had my best clothes on and wouldn't run any risk. But your father is laying for it with a club.

Har. I don't envy him his job.

Mar. [*Calls, off.*] Oh, Harry, come and see if you can git this winder down, it's stuck.

Har. All right, mother, I'll fix it. [*Ex. R. D. Hammering heard and slamming of window.*]

Elsie. [c.] Will, I want to thank you.

Will. [*Sitting L. of table.*] For what?

Elsie. For the sacrifice you are prepared to make. Harry has told me, and I know what it means. If he is unable to get this money you intend to give him your savings, and deny yourself the schooling for which you have struggled so long and hard.

Will. Not *deny* myself the schooling—only postpone it—for Harry will pay me back every cent as quickly as possible. The boy is honest, but he has been led away by bad company.

Elsie. It is still a great sacrifice. It would be a generous, a noble thing to do for your own brother; and Harry is a stranger to you.

Will. Now, don't say another word. He will most probably get the money from your father, and in that case all your thanks will be entirely thrown away.

Elsie. No—your intention is just the same. [*Goes a little R.*] Oh, Will, I know you are doing this for my sake, and it makes me feel mean and contemptible that I can only give you gratitude in return.

Will. Believe me, Elsie, if I thought your love could be bought with a price like this I would not pay it. [*Rises.*]

Elsie. [R. C.] I hoped you would feel that way about it—indeed, I knew you would. I shall always look upon you as my dearest friend.

Will. And I shall always look upon you as my dearest—well, no matter what; but the reflection that while there is life there is hope is a cheering one.

Elsie. Truly, Will, I do not wish to wound you, but it will be wiser to forget me. You will find some one more worthy of you and with whom you can be happy.

Will. There is but one woman in the world for me, and if I don't win her it will not be my fault. [*Takes her hand.*] May I keep on trying? May I, Elsie?

Elsie. Ouch! I have a sore finger on that hand—would you mind using the other? [*Harry re-enters.*]

Will. Oh, I beg your pardon. [*Takes the other hand.*]

Har. [*Up R.*] Mother wants you, Elsie. [**Will** *crosses hurriedly to* c.] Oh, excuse me—I didn't mean to intrude.

Elsie. You are not intruding—not in the least. [*Ex. R. door in a pet.*]

Har. [*Comes down.*] I say, Bill, that looked like remarkably close friendship.

Will. [c.] That is all it amounts to. She cares nothing for me, and has just told me so. [*Crosses R.*]

Ezra. [*Off D. I. F.*] Oh, Bill—Harry—hello—

Har. [L. c. *Calling.*] What's the matter, dad, have you killed it? [*Goes up a little c.*]

Ezra. [*Sticks head in at door.*] Dead as a smelt. But, oh, gosh, how lively it smelt after it was dead. Say, no gals around, is they?

Har. No one here but Bill and me.

Ezra. Then I'll come in. [*Enters in a barrel. Comes down to L. door.*]

Har. For heaven's sake, dad! What's the matter?

Ezra. I killed the skunk, but had to bury my clothes. [*Ex. L. and then sticks head out.*] I'll never be able to wear them pants again. [*Disappears. Same buss.*] Bill, you can have that coat and vest if you like to dig for 'em. [*Same buss.*] But, say, Bill, I wouldn't disturb them pants if I was you, unless you've got your life insured. [*Same buss.*] Harry, go and ast your maw whether she has any musk or ile of peppermint. If she hain't, you git me some asafidity and creosote, or even a couple of last season's eggs and the kerosene can. Any old smell will be better than this.

Har. I'd better get you a box of lye and a scrubbing brush.

Ezra. You don't say so. Mebbe I'd better use sapolio. [*Ezra closes door.* Harry *goes up and ex. R. laughing.*]

Zach. [*Enters D. I. F. after knocking. Carries umbrella.*] Good evening. Is Brother Meeker at home? [*Coming down.*]

Will. [*Down R.*] He is.

Zach. Will you kindly tell him I'd like to see him?

Will. [*Crosses and knocks at door L.*] Mr. Meeker, Mr. Smarden would like to see you.

Ezra. [*Off L. door.*] You don't say so. I reckon he'd better not just now, unless he's got on blinders.

Will. [*To Zach.*] He has just killed a skunk, and is cleaning up after it. [*Goes up.*]

Zach. Oh, indeed. I thought I noticed a peculiar odor. I am not in any hurry. I'll wait. [*Ex. Will R.*]

Mar. [*Entering R.*] Why, Brother Smarden, what brings you here?

Zach. [*Down R. C.*] I have come to make one final plea to

Brother Meeker in behalf of Christian morals and public decency.
I trust we are not overheard? [*Sits in rocker.*]
Mar. Oh, no—the doors are shut. [*Comes down.*]
Zach. After much prayer and earnest discussion, Sister
Meeker, it has been given to us that it is the Lord's will that we
should proceed to aggressive measures. This is a Christian na-
tion, sister, yet the authorities, for selfish and corrupt ends, refuse
to maintain the majesty of the people's laws.
Mar. [c.] The very words I said to Ezra not an hour ago.
Zach. Therefore, all who obstruct the onward march of reform
by refusing to give heed to argument, must be compelled to do so
by force.
Mar. [*Crosses and sits L. of table.*] That's Ezra. He can't
argey. He always gits mad. But he says we'll git into the penitentiary if they's any whippin's.
Zach. Those of us who are sanctified, Sister Meeker, can never
more commit sin. We are merely instruments in the Lord's
hands. Why, if you or I should blow up the saloon with gunpowder or dynamite it would only be a manifestation of the
workings of divine providence, and we would run no danger. The
Lord will protect his chosen instruments.
Mar. I have my thirds in that saloon propity, and that's what
hurts my conscience so. If they was to explode it they could
blow in my share and welcome.
Zach. Noble woman! Ah, Sister Meeker, yours is one of the
loveliest characters I have ever known. If all Christians were as
full of earnest faith our beloved country would not this night be
groaning under the heel of the tyrant rum.
Mar. I'm one of them what believes in works as well as words.
[*Hitching her chair closer.*] Now, say, supposin' I touched off a
dynamite cattridge under that place myself—hain't I got a right
to? It's partly mine.
Zach. If the spirit moved you to do so you would be justified.
It is clear that the Lord intends Lem Davis to be driven out of
this community.
Mar. Well, they's dynamite out in the barn, and the men are
goin' stumpin' to-morrer. I reckon I'll kinder watch 'em and see
how they set it off.
Zach. Not of your own free will, sister—only if the spirit
moves you, after praying for guidance.
Pickles. [*Enters R.*] Oh, Miss Meeker, could you come here
a minute?
Mar. What is it now? [*Rising. Sharply.*] Excuse, me,
Brother Smarden. [*Goes up.*]

Zach. Certainly. [*He rises. Ex. Mar. R.*] This woman shall
be the instrument of my revenge. She shall rid me of Lem
Davis, for one of us must leave town. If he remains it will only
be a matter of a few days or weeks until he will be able to prove
me an impostor. Then farewell to all my dreams of notoriety and
wealth. I must be prepared for flight—I must have money.
Money enough to put the sea between me and my past, if need
be. [*Goes up.*]

Ezra. [*Entering L. followed by* **Harry.**] No sir-ree Bob! Let
you take two hundred dollars without security? I think I see
myself. [*Crossing R.*]

Har. [*Following him across.*] But, father, it is perfectly
safe —I will give you my own note.

Ezra. Who can you git to back it?

Har. Why—I could get Bill—Bill Goodall—

Ezra. [*Sits in rocker. Laughs.*] Say, sonny, the bank would
not give five cents on the thousand dollars for them two signa-
tures. No, no—folks that is honest and able to pay their debts
don't have to pay no twenty-four per cent when its durn hard to
git six if the security's good.

Har. [R. C.] My friend will lose everything if I don't get the
money. Won't you let me take it, father? [*Very nervous and
excited.*]

Ezra. Not on your autograph. You hain't responsible or
you'd have two hundred dollars, and more, saved outen sixty dollars a month by this time.

Har. [*Aside. Going.*] Refused—and I was so certain of it!
Now for Lem Davis. [*Ex. D. I. E.*]

Zach. [*Aside.*] That boy is in trouble. Two hundred dollars
is the amount. I'll make a mental note of that. [*Aloud.*] Good
evening, Brother Meeker. [*Comes down C.*]

Ezra. [*Gruffly.*] Good evenin'. What do *you* want?

Zach. To make one final effort in the Lem Davis matter.

Ezra. You don't say so. Then I tell you candidly you may
save your words, for my mind's made up. Some of your crowd
has been writin' me a threatenin' letter, and if I find out who it
is they'll be trouble. [*Rocks himself angrily.*]

Zach. [C.] I know nothing about that.

Ezra. You don't say so. [*Rises.*] Looks like you'd come
a-purpose to gimme my last chance afore the whitecaps gits me.
[**Lem** *enters D. I. E. unseen.*]

Zach. You are quite mistaken. I know nothing about either
letter or whitecaps. [*Goes L.*]

Ezra. [*Has been searching among papers taken from pocket.*

Crosses L. C.] Well, there's the letter. [*Hands it.*] The white-caps ain't arrived yet, but you'll mebbe be among 'em when they come.

Zach. [L. *Aside.*] Soper's writing, badly disguised. [*Aloud.*] You are doing me a terrible injustice. To prove it I will keep this letter, and if anything occurs I will aid the law in running down the perpetrators.

Ezra. You don't say so. Well, I guess not. [*Snatches letter.*] I'll take care of that letter myself.

Zach. Your suspicions are absurd.

Ezra. I wouldn't put it apast you bein' the head of the hull *conspiracy*, for I believe you are jest what Lem Davis says you are—a fraud and an imposture. [*Crosses* R.]

Zach. [L.] Lem Davis shall repent that slander. I am going to make him prove his words. [**Mar.** *enters as* **Lem.** *comes down and drops down* L. C.]

Lem. [C. *Coming down.*] Which he will do as soon as you choose. Your pretended references have been written to, and answers will git back in a few days along with your photo from the rogues' gallery.

Zach. I'll give you plenty of chance to produce those letters in court, besides answering several other charges.

Mar. [L. C.] Lem Davis, I want you to git right outen this house this minute. There's the door—scoot. [*Furiously angry.*]

Ezra. [R.] Stop right where you are, Lemuel; don't pay no attention to her at all. This homestead is mine.

Mar. Don't you believe it. I'm a-runnin' this house, and its as much mine as yourn.

Ezra. [*Takes stage.* **Lem.** *drops down* R. *côrner.*] You've been runnin' things round here for the last thirty years, Mariar, and your time's up. From this day forth I'm boss—do you hear me? I'm *boss!*

Mar. [*Up to him.*] Not while *I* live, you old sinner, you. Ain't you ashamed of yourself, to act like a dog before——

Ezra. Shet up! [*Shouting.*] Shet up, I tell you. From this time forth I don't want to hear nothin' from you but silence.

Zach. Let this contention cease. I am the innocent cause of it and I will go. Good night, Sister Meeker. I will pray for your husband. [*Goes up.*]

Ezra. You don't say so. Much obliged. Hold on--don't you want your umbrel? [*Picks up umbrella.* **Mar.** *takes it and hands it to* **Zach.**] Say, you might pray a few for Mariar. I don't know anybody 'at needs it wuss.

Zach. Get thee behind me, satan. [*Ex.* D. I. F. **Mar.** *closes* *door and ex. R. Zach. is seen watching through window during entire scene.*]

Lem. I came mighty nigh picking that mug up and pitchin' him through the winder. [*Sits R. of table.*]

Ezra. Just as well you didn't, Lem. Let all the violence come from the other side and then we've got 'em.

Lem. Mebbe you're right. Well, let's settle up   *Mar. and Elsie enter R. with* **Will.**]

Ezra. [*Sitting at small table R. with* **Lem.**] Hello, where you all goin'?

Elsie. Only over to Deacon Soper's, father. We'll not be long. [*The three ex. D. I. F.*]

Lem. Over to Soper's, eh? I met a hull crowd of the tempernce push on the way there as I came in. What's up?

Ezra. Oh, some Bible class or prayer meetin' or kissin' match or somethin'. But let's get down to business. [**Zach.** *very attentive at window.*]

Lem. Well, here's the bills for the month—here's the statement—and it shows your share to be two hundred and four dollars and fifty cents.

Ezra. [*Glancing through bills, etc.*] You don't say so. And them people atchilly think they can make me a dry when I'm makin' fifty dollars a week by bein' wet? [**Lem.** *is counting money.*] Say, Lem, how on earth can you keep bar and keep sober?

Lem. By letting my customers do all the drinking—I never touch it.

Ezra. You don't say so. You're too smart to run any chances with liquor, eh?' Me too. I don't even know the taste of it.

Lem. And you don't want to learn, neither. Say, I sell whiskey, and have sold it all my life, but I'd sooner see that boy of mine in his coffin than in front of a bar with a glass of liquor in his hand.

Ezra. Folks 'at drinks is a passel of fools 'at don't know the value of money or they wouldn't be so durn reckless in makin' themselves poor to make us rich. But somebody is goin' to sell liquor so long's it's made, and it might as well be us as some other fellers. Eh, Lemuel?

Lem. Fact—a heap sight better. Here, count this. [**Ezra** *counts.*] I don't allow no drunks in my place, 'cept Jaggsy, and he's bound to git drunk anyhow when he takes the notion.

Ezra. This is all right. [*Gets cashbox in dresser drawer R. and puts money in it.*] I suppose trade has dropped down, since the spazzum began, tremenjus.

Lem. Well, I should say. All the better element, as they call
'em, that used to take their toddy on the sly, has quit.

Ezra. [*Putting cash box in drawer of dresser R.*] Oh, well,
they'll all come round again when the reform wave flops back.

Lem. Sure thing. Well, I'm off. [*Rising.*]

Ezra. I'll go a piece of the way with you. [*Goes up to D. I F.*
Zach. *disappears.*] Mebbe I'll go over to Soper's and kinder nose
round a bit to see what's goin' on. [*Ex. with Lem. D. I. F. Zach.
enters D. I. F.*]

Zach. [*Tiptoes to door R. and looks off. Closes door.*] The
girl is sound asleep curled up in a chair. There is not a soul to
disturb me. [*Lays umbrella on table C. Gets cash box.*] Now
if I have a key that will fit. Let me see. [*Tries two or three
keys.*] At last. [*Opens cash box at table C. and takes money.*]
Now, Lem Davis, do your worst—I am ready to fight or retreat,
whichever prudence may dictate. [*Puts cash box back in drawer.
Puts money in wallet. Ex. D. I. F.*]

Pickles. [*Enters R. rubbing eyes.*] I thought I heard somebody here—sounded as if they was rattlin' a tin box or unlockin'
somethin'. Reckon I must a dreamed it. [*Comes down.*] Oh, I
wish to gracious I was back in the poor house—it's a picnic com-
pared to this. The paupers are a nice, sociable crowd. But here
I'm so dead sleepy by the time I git through my work I can't en-
joy myself a bit. Reckon I'll go to bed. [*Sees umbrella.*] Hello,
Smarden's forgot his umbershoot—ain't it a daisy. [*Opens it,
parades, etc.*] I dassen't swipe it, but I'll put it away nice and
careful in my closet till he comes after it—and I hope he'll forget
to come. [*Closes umbrella.* **Har.** *enters D. I. F.*] Sakes alive! I
thought you was over to Deacon Soper's. [*Hiding umbrella behind her.*]

Har. No, I didn't go with them. [*Coming down R. C.*]

Pick. [L. C.] Well, you didn't miss much. I went to one of
them sociables once to help with supper, and they made soup for
forty-one head outen two quarts of oysters and a gallon of milk.
When we served it it was a case of Billy, Billy button, who's got
the oyster?

Har. Pretty thin stew, Pickles.

Pick. Yes, but you ought to a seen the coffee and the ham
sangwiches. Say, that ham was cut so thin you could see to read
through it, and the coffee was poorer than I be—Lord knows
that's poor enough. Well, good night. [*Going R.*]

Har. Good night, Pickles. [*Ex.* **Pick.** R. *He walks nervously to and fro.*] Everything is against me. The saloon is closed

and Lem is nowhere to be found. I'm as nervous as a cat. [**Will**
enters D. I. F.]

Will. Hello, Harry.

Har. [L. C. *Startled.*] What—you here, Bill? I thought you
went to the sociable.

Will. [*Coming down.*] So I did, but I sneaked away again,
so as to have a grind at the law of evidence. Why didn't you go?

Har. I went to see Davis. Dad has refused to help me.

Will. [R. C. *down.*] How about Davis?

Har. The saloon is closed, so I didn't see him. I tell you
what, I'm desperate!

Will. Don't give up. Have a good sleep and get after him to-
morrow.

Har. A good sleep? I haven't had that in two weeks. That's
what makes me so nervous. Well, I'm going upstairs.

Will. All right, I'm going to read. [*Ex.* **Har.** L. I. E. *Gets
law book, which is held in valise strap.*] How queer he looked—
as if he had been caught doing something. I don't think he'll be
apt to go astray again. His conscience troubles him too much
and he'll never forget how it feels to be guilty of a crime and on
the verge of exposure. [*Sits* L. *of table down* L. *and opens book.*
Ezra *enters* D. 1. F.]

Ezra. Hello, Bill—got home early, didn't ye?

Will. Yes; it was pretty slow, and I thought I could use the
time to better advantage. I don't believe Mrs. Meeker'll stay
very long, either.

Ezra. Why so? [*Coming down* R. C.]

Will. Oh, Mrs. Balmer was there, of course, and they hadn't
been together five minutes before she did or said something that
put Mrs. Meeker in a temper. She would have come home right
away if Elsie hadn't persuaded her that it would look bad.

Ezra. I swan, to see them two weemin together is more fun'n
a cat fight. Well, seein's you're here and I got the money mebbe
we'd better settle up. How much is comin' to you? [*Going up
to dresser.*]

Will. There was a balance of seven dollars for last month and
fifty cents for the dynamite—twenty-seven fifty—that squares us.

Ezra. [*Stops and turns half way up.*] Hold on, Bill--hold on.
I have an offset agin' that.

Will. I don't remember it.

Ezra. [*Coming down a little.*] Don't you remember the four-
teen cents I paid for your laundry and the two stamps I loaned
you? [**Mar.** *and* **Elsie** *enter* D. F. *and come down* L. C.]

Will. Why, yes— I had forgotten about that eighteen cents. But there's a dollar fifty for to-morrow.

Ezra. A dollar fifty? Didn't I say a dollar, Bill?

Will. Indeed you didn't.

Ezra. I thought I said a dollar.

Elsie. [L.] No, father— it was a dollar fifty. I heard you.

Ezra. My mistake—I meant to say a dollar. Well, I'll pay you that to-morrow night when your work is done. I might as as well save the interest on a dollar'n a half as give it to you. [*Goes to dresser.*] That's twenty-seven dollars and thirty-two cents you want.

Will. That's right. You didn't stop long at the party, Mrs. Meeker.

Mar. [L. C.] Well, har'ly. Not after the way that Martha Strong acted. Ezra, tho Rev. Mrs. Balmer atchilly turned up her nose at *me*.

Ezra. [*At dresser* R.] You don't say so. Well, if Martha improved on nature any, after what nature has done in turnin' up her snout, she must a looked a sight. [*Unlocks cash box and finds money gone.*] Hello—what's the meanin' of this? Where's that roll of bills? I put it there and locked the box—and it's gone—gone—two hundred and four dollars and fifty cents. Why I—I don't understand it—I've been robbed—robbed of two hundred and four dollars and fifty cents. [*Coming down* C. *with cash box.*]

Mar. Robbed? You're crazy, Ezra, they hain't no robbers been here—look again.

Ezra. [*Rummaging in box.*] It's gone—gone I tell ye—who could a done it? [*Pause.*] I know the robber, by gracious! [*Calls.*] Harry—Harry! [**Elsie** *crosses* R.]

Har. [*Off* L.] What is it, father?

Ezra. Come here—I want ye. [**Harry** *enters* L. I. E. *in shirt sleeves.*]

Har. What's the matter. [L. C.]

Ezra. [C.] Matter? Don't you dast to ask me what's the matter. Where's them two hundred and four dollars and fifty cents? [**Will** *and* **Elsie** R. *corner*, **Mar.** L.]

Har. I don't know what you mean. Which two hundred and four dollars and fifty cents?

Ezra. That you stole outen that cash box while I was gone a piece with Lem Davis.

Har. *I* stole money from your cash box? Why, father—you are surely not in earnest!

Ezra. Yes, I am in earnest. Do you think I'm a fool? Do

you think I didn't see clear through it when you was so dead anxious to borry two hundred dollars at twenty-four per cent interest for a friend of yours? Well, I did. You wanted that money for yourself, to help you outen some devilment you've gotten into in the city. That's what you wanted it for, and that's why you didn't have money of your own after earnin' sixty dollars a month for more'n a year. Now give it up! [*Throws cash box* R.]

Mar. [*Crosses to* **Ezra**, **Har**. *drops down to* L. *corner*.] Ezra Meeker, hain't you ashamed? To try and make your own son out a thief!

Ezra. Don't you mix up in this, Mariar, or you'll wish you hadn't. Now, then, Henery Ward Meeker, I'll just give you one minute to produce that money, and if you don't I'll put you through for it as sure as my name's Ezra. [*Turns to go up.* **Mar.** *holds him back.*]

Har. Father, I swear I know nothing about it. I never saw the money, never touched it. [**Mar.** *argues with* **Ezra** *in pantomime, drawing him* L.]

Elsie. [*Aside to* **Will.**] Will, if you love me, do something to save him.

Will. [R. C.] I will, for your sake, but I doubt if he is worth it.

Elsie. He was not himself—he was unbalanced by worry and excitement. Do something—anything—to gain time and give him one more chance.

Har. [*Crosses* R. C.] Elsie—Will—you know all—but surely you do not believe me guilty of this? [*Tries to take* **Elsie's** *hand.* **Will** *stops him.*]

Will. [*Aside.*] Stop—don't dare to soil your sister with that hand—it is stained with crime. [*Aloud, going* C.] Mr. Meeker, I will restore your money. It was taken under great temptation, and I can only say that I am sorry—bitterly sorry—that the crime was committed. [*Takes money from wallet and hands it to* **Ezra.**]

Ezra. [L. C.] What! you, Bill Goodall—a thief? [**Will** *bows head and turns away.*]

Elsie. [*Crossing to him* R. C.] No—no. Will—not that—not that. [*Sobbing.*]

Will. [C. *Aside.*] Hush—it is the only way to save him.

Mar. [L.] What did I tell you, Ezra? What did I tell you? Didn't I say I wouldn't trust him no further than I could fling a bull by the tail? [**Har.** *sits* R. *of table, despairingly.*]

Ezra. [*Has been counting money.*] Hush up, will ye, Mariar? If anybody had a-told me this about you, Bill, I'd a called 'em a liar, if I had to fight for it. Here's your wages. You can keep them eighteen cents, and I reckon I'll make out to do the stumpin' to-morrer without your help. [*Goes* L.]

Mar. Mebbe you'll listen to me next time, Ezra. I told you to give Bill his walkin' papers long ago, or you'd be sorry for it.

Ezra. You don't say so. [*Ex.* L.]

Mar. Yes, I *do* say so, and *did* say so. [*To* **Will.**] Now, young man you'll have to travel. They hain't no room in this house for you. Christian families and robbers don't sorter mix together right.

Elsie. [R.] Mother—[*Protesting and appealing.*]

Mar. [L. C.] Not one word, darter. Mebbe you'll trust your mother after this. I warned you agin this feller when I first see him hangin' round you. Well, this is a judgment on me for not wrastlin' powerful enough with your paw over the saloon, I suppose. Now, then, are you goin' to travel?

Will. [R. C.] I am. [*Crosses* L. *Picks up valise.*] Charity does not seem to be one of *your* Christian virtues, Mrs. Meeker.

Mar. I hain't got no charity to waste on cattle like you. [*Goes up and opens* D. I. F.]

Elsie. [*Meeting* **Will** C. *Aside, taking his hand.*] Forgive her, Will—she does not know—and—I love you.

Will. God bless you, dear.

Mar. Now, then, out you git—[*Ex.* **Will** D. I. F. **Elsie** *crying* L. *of table*]—and a good riddance to bad rubbish.

Elsie. Oh, Harry, Harry! I loved and trusted you so, and this is all through you.

Har. I didn't make him do it.

Elsie. Didn't make him do it—what base ingratitude! [*Rising.*] I'm disgusted with you. [*Ex.* R. *crying.* **Mar.** *locking door, etc.*]

Mar. Good night, Elsie. Don't ye cry, now—he hain't worth it. [*Aside.*] Couldn't a been no nicer if I'd a planned it myself. With Bill outen the way she'll listen to Brother Smarden, and she'll marry him, too.

Har. [*Aside.*] Well, [*rising*] this cuts off my last resource if Davis refuses. What a hypocrite the fellow is—to preach to me at the very moment he was laying his plans to get me out of my scrape by robbing Dad! [*Going* L.]

Mar. [*Coming down.*] Harry, your paw's got to apologize to you in the mornin' or I leave this house. The idear of chargin' you with robbin' him. Why, you wouldn't take a pin 'at wasn't yours. Well, good night, son—don't forget your prayers. [*Kisses him.*]

Har. Good night, mother. [*Ex. R. I. E.*]

Mar. [*Looking toward window.*] I'm sorry the lock on that window is broke. I'll have Ezra fix it to-morrer. Now, I think I've tended to everything. If I don't see to things myself they hain't never done. [*Puts out light, stage darkens and ex. R. Whitecaps appear at window and throw light from bullseye lantern into room.*]

Soper. [*Outside window.*] They're in bed, brethren. Now make no noise. How can we get in?

First Whitecap. [Zach.] Knock on the door and he'll open it. Then we've got him.

Soper. That won't do. The old fox is too crafty for that.

First Whitecap. Then try the window.

Soper. [*Tries window.*] It's all right—it will open. Now get in quietly. [*He opens window and they get in. All come down stage.*] Well, brethren, we're in. The next thing is to get him out of his room.

First Whitecap. [R. C.] Throw something down and make a noise. That'll scare him out. [*Other whitecaps grouped around from R. C. to L. C.*]

Soper. [C.] Yes, scare him out of the winder. Can't you think of something better than that? [Ezra *enters with shotgun L. door, and goes unseen up stage where he hides behind ironing on clothes horse.*]

First Whitecap. We know where he sleeps. If he hain't got his door locked let's pull him outen his bed.

Soper. That's better. You get him, brethren, and I'll whip him. I'll lay it on right good, too.

Ezra. [*Throws down clothes horse.*] You don't say so. Throw up your hands every dirty, low, measly skunk of ye or I'll punch your tickets to the bad place with buckshot. I will, by gracious. [*Calls.*] Harry—oh, Harry! fetch a light!

Har. I'm coming, father. [*Enters L. I. E. with light. Stage is lighted. He crosses it and places on table R.*]

Ezra. Don't you move till I tell ye, dad gast ye. I've got both bar'ls loaded to the muzzle, and after shootin' through the South for four long years, you can bet your pants I hain't skeered of burnin' powder.

Soper. [C.] I want to go home. [Har. *goes up R.*]

Ezra. You don't say so. Well, you will when I'm through with you.

First Whitecap. We are in a trap.

Ezra. [*Goes C. half way down.*] Regular hornet's nest. Now, you first rooster—you—come up here and lay down that whip right on this spot. If either of you other temperance reformers offers to move I'll let fly, and I shouldn't wonder if I git the whole of you at one flop. [*White caps bring up whips and lay them down. Ad lib. dialogue.*] Now, Harry, you pick out the handiest one of them whips.

Har. This is a good one, father. [*Hands stuffed whip.*]

Ezra. [*Comes down* [c.] Put the others in my room there and lock the door. [*Harry carries whips off* L. *door.*] I'm goin' to give you gents a sample of how it feels to git whitecapped. I I hain't goin' to try to find out who you are nor take the law onto you. I'm just agoin' to give you the dose of gospel temperance reform you tried to give me, and don't forgit that breakin' into a man's house at dead of night with a mask on gives that man a right by law to shoot you dead. [**Har.** *returns.*] Now, Harry, you take that gun, and the first one that makes a break at me gits the right bar'l.

Har. [L.] He'll get it, father. [*Puts gun to shoulder.*]

Ezra. Pray, gents, pray. This is a Christian temperance convention. Now, if you've prayed enough, dance, durn ye, dance. [*Sails in and whips them. They howl, go on knees and beg for mercy, etc.*] I'll gin you mercy, dod rat you. That's one for luck, etc. [*Ad lib.* **Pick.**, **Elsie** *and* **Mar.** *come to entrance and group up* R.] Dance, durn you, dance. [*Whipping them.*]

Curtain.

ACT III.

[*Scene. A street with set saloon, obliqued across* L. *upper corner. Sign over door, "Cigars—* **Lem Davis** *—Billiards." Door and window in saloon, to flip and break away at explosion. Barrels and kegs in front of saloon. At rise* **Zach.** *and* **Deacon** *enter* R. *Bench* C. *with set fountain, statue or big flower urn back of it.*]

Deacon. [*Lame and using a stick. Shade over one eye.*] Oh, Brother Smarden, such a surprise as we got! Either it was not the Lord's will that we should whip Ezra Meeker, or the devil turned in and helped him powerful. Look at me—I'm a wreck. [*Sits on bench* C.]

Zach. [R. C.] Oh, thou of little faith! Don't you know that whom the Lord loveth he chasteneth?

Deacon. Well, I got chastened. I have wales on my back and legs, a twisted ankle and a black eye. Oh, Brother Smarden, how I suffer! [*Groans and rubs himself.*]

Zach. Keep on with the good work, brother. Those who wish to wear the crown must bear the cross, you know. How about the other brother?

Deacon. He is laid up, too. Oh, Brother Smarden, Ezra is a terrible man when he is aroused. I wouldn't tackle him again to whip him—not for a farm. [*Groans.*]

Zach. You hadn't the courage to enter till I led you, and but for your cowardice we would have whipped him. We must turn our attention to Lem Davis next time.

Deacon. But no whipping—no, sir. [*Half whispering.*] I'll help blow up his place, or burn it down, or anything else to drive him away, but I've had all the whitecapping I can stand. [*Groans.*]

Zach. You have borne your share of the heat and burden of the day in that direction, But there is something else that you can and must do.

Deacon. What is that, brother?

Zach. This man Davis has written to his friends to send him letters damaging my character and assailing my integrity. Those letters must be stopped—they must never reach him.

Deacon. How can it be prevented?

Zach. You are the postmaster. [*Bending over and speaking with intention.*]

Deacon. What! Me stop letters in the mail? [*Rises, frightened.*] Oh, Brother Smarden, my conscience wouldn't let me. [*Crosses L.* **Zach.** *follows him.*] I'm afraid I'd get caught.

Zach. Look at me—look at me in the eye. [*Walks backward and* **Deacon** *follows, fascinated, to bench, where he drops limply.*] You will not get caught, for this is only a means to foil a conspiracy against the Lord's work. Don't you feel it is so, Brother Soper? [*Very intensely.*]

Deacon. Ye'—yes—it—it must be done. Oh, yes—as you say —it is to help the cause. I'll bring all the letters to you, Brother Smarden, indeed I will.

Zach. That is right. Now go to your office. [*Pointing L.*]

Deacon. Yes, yes—it must be done—there is no danger in doing the Lord's work. [*Ex. L. I. E. as if dazed, muttering to himself.*]

Zach. [*Watching him off.*] Again the strong mind dominates the weak one. I could compel that poor fool to do anything, now, even to committing murder. [*Crosses R. in thought.*]

Mar. [*Entering* R. I. E.] Oh, Brother Smarden, such news! Everythin' is all agoin' reg'lar skewgee. [*Flops into bench.*]

Zach. [R. C.] What is the matter, sister?

Mar. Why, hain't you heard about the whitecaps tryin' to git Ezra last night?

Zach. Yes, I did hear something of it.

Mar. Well, Ezra got *them*, and you never see such an all-fired whippin' as he gave 'em in all your born days. When Mayor Spraddlin' heard of it, what d'you suppose he done?

Zach. I haven't heard.

Mar. Called a special meetin' of the council. They've offered one hundred dollars reward for the arrest of the whitecaps, and the order closin' Lem Davis up has been withdrawed. Ain't it awful?

Zach. The Lord will raise up an instrument to close it again with fire and smoke and total destruction.

Mar. Amen, Brother Smarden—amen to that. Ezra got robbed, too, last night afore the whitecaps come.

Zach. Robbed? Who robbed him?

Mar. He told me not to tell [*rises and goes* R. *to* Zach. *confidentially*], but I look on you as my pasture now, and I feel it's my duty to. 'Twas our hired man, Bill Goodall. Yes, sir; robbed Ezra of two hundred and four dollars and fifty cents, and when Ezra accused our Harry of taking it, and said he'd put him through, Bill's conscience hurt him that bad that he up and confessed and gave back the money.

Zach. [*Aside.*] Bill Goodall confessed and gave back the money? What can this mean?

Mar. Bill was all ready to skip to Chicago, but I guess he hain't agoin' now.

Zach. I am glad that your son was cleared of all suspicion.

Mar. Yes, indeed, Brother Smarden. Why, that boy wouldn't steal if he was starvin'. But, say, it was good another way—it gits rid of Bill. If I was you, Brother Smarden, I'd kinder call round and see Elsie. [*Sits on bench.*]

Zach. I shall do so, Sister Meeker. I admire your daughter very much, and I have been thinking over what you said about a married missionary having more influence.

Spraddling. [*Enters* R. I. E.] Good day to you.

Mar. Good day, Mayor Spraddlin'. Did you git through?

Sprad. Yes; we've adjourned. [*Crossing* L. C.]

Zach. [*Leaning against back of bench* C.] I hope you and the aldermen have been guided aright in your action, Mr. Mayor.

Sprad. I believe we have, Mr. Smarden. The dastardly outrage attempted last night has opened the eyes of some people who didn't believe that the fanatics of the temperance party would attempt violence.

Zach. Desperate diseases require desperate remedies, Mr. Mayor--not that I fully approve of the affair of last night.

Sprad. The man who does approve of that is nothing better than an anarchist.

Zach. Then you believe in enforcing the law?

Sprad. I do.

Zach. And you will keep this grog shop closed?

Sprad. Not necessarily.

Zach. But you will if you enforce the law, Mr. Mayor.

Sprad. We must use discretion. The sentiment of the public must govern that—and public opinion is against the desperate men who have openly threatened to proceed to dynamite and fire. That is mob rule and anarchy pure and simple.

Zach. [*Coming down to him.*] To tell the truth, Mr. Mayor, the brewers and the whisky trust have plenty of money, and are willing to spend it freely to purchase action favorable to their traffic, and to pay advocates who will bolster up their infamous business with talk about mob rule and anarchy.

Sprad. Stop--you have gone too far. Even your cloth shall not protect you if you repeat that slanderous inuendo. If you have any evidence to back the charges you insinuate, go before the grand jury and make them openly. [*Going* L.]

Mar. [*Rises.*] We can't do it, Ben Spraddlin', because the bribers is too sharp to let us catch 'em. But you hain't runnin' politics in this town merely for your health, and you know it.

Ezra. [*Entering* L.] You don't say so. An' you hain't agaddin' round town, attendin' meetin's and makin' yourself a general nuisance, neglectin' your housework and makin' me go without supper for *my* health, neither.

Mar. [*Down* C.] I've been your slave long enough, Ezra Meeker. If you want supper Pickles can git it for you. It is my mission to work in the temperance cause, and I'm agoin' to do it for all you.

Ezra. [*Goes* C. *to her.*] If some of you weemin' would reform your tempers, reform your cookin', reform the way you treat your hired help, and reform your ideas that you're the whole thing, you'd be in better business. [*Sits* C.]

Sprad. [L.] Now you're talking sense, Ezra. This woman business is a perfect craze. They insist upon neglecting the duties plainly imposed upon them by nature, to invade business and public life as man's rival. There is scarcely a thing men do that they don't attempt.

Mar. [R. C.] 'Cept chaw terbacker, drink liquor and hold out their hands for boodle.

Ezra. You don't say so. Just give 'em time and they'll do all that and more, too.

Zach. [L. C.] Woman in this civilized age is no longer the slave, but the equal of man.

Ezra. You don't say so. I'll bet Mariar's the equal of any three men—to hear her tell it. Hello—here comes Lem, and he's in a hurry. [*Lem enters* R. 2 E.] Howdy, Lem—where you goin' so fast?

Lem. [R. C.] Howdy. I'm just goin' to open up.

Sprad. The aldermen say they'd sooner see one place run wide open than a dozen blind pigs on the sly.

Lem. Bully! Come in and take somethin'. Come on, Ezra, I want to show you them leaky pipes. [*Ex. with* **Ezra** *and* **Sprad.** *into saloon after unlocking door.*]

Mar. [C.] It's a wonder to me that man wa'n't struck down dead.

Zach. He will be visited yet. Oh, that the chief magistrate should enter such a place! [*Sits* C.]

Mar. Say, Brother Smarden, I see them blowin' up them stumps this mornin'. [*Sitting beside him.*]

Zach. A very interesting operation, Sister Meeker.

Mar. An' I know how to set off dynamite now.

Zach. Knowledge is power, sister.

Mar. An' I have a stick of it and a cap an' fuse hid under the dooryard step, Brother Smarden.

Zach. An excellent place to store them, Sister Meeker. Dynamite should never be kept indoors, especially near the fire.

Mar. I reckon one stick 'ud about bust up that saloon business, Brother Smarden.

Zach. If it were properly placed and exploded it doubtless would, Sister Meeker.

Mar. An' it hain't sinful to root out evil doers, Brother Smarden?

Zach. David went forth and slew the enemies of the Lord, Sister Meeker.

Mar. And they can't do anything to a person for blowin' up their own propity, can they, Brother Smarden?

Zach. We may do as we will with our own, Sister Meeker.

Mar. [*Rises.*] Then I bar the saloon as my thirds of all Ezra's got, Brother Smarden.

Zach. [*Rising.*] Pray that you may use your property for the good of mankind, Sister Meeker, and I will pray for you, also. I shall call on Elsie this evening. Good bye, Sister Meeker. [*Ex.* R.]

Mar. That dear good man! He as good as told me to do it. I would, too, if I wasn't skeered of gittin' caught. Ezra'd almost kill me if he found out. Oh, I wisht I only dast to do it. [*Ex.* L.]

Elsie. [*Enters with* **Will** R. 2 E.] Harry remains as stubborn as can be, and declares that he had nothing to do with taking the money. I have tried to persuade him to confess several times, but he only gets angry and says you took it. [*Sits* C.]

Will. [R. C.] It is hard to believe that a boy apparently so frank would act as he is doing. Yet the circumstances are so strongly against him that it is almost impossible to think otherwise.

Elsie. Could anybody else have stolen it?

Will. Pickles was the only one in the house after your father left with Davis, and it is absurd to think of her as the thief.

Elsie. I have questioned her. She fell asleep, she says, and I am satisfied that she knows nothing about it.

Will. Elsie, I am convinced that Harry is telling the truth.

Elsie. I feel inclined to believe him, too, especially as he has remained here to try to raise the two hundred dollars, instead of going back to Chicago.

Will. That is just the point that struck me. If he had taken that money he would have gone back to-day.

Elsie. I know that he saw Davis early in the afternoon.

Will. With what result?

Elsie. Lem said he hadn't the money by him, but if the mayor let him reopen he would try to give it to him to-morrow.

Will. How does your father take it?

Elsie. He kept his eyes on Harry all the time he was speaking and said, "Bill is a good fellow, if he did make a mistake."

Will. My mind is made up. I'll not leave here until this thing is explained and the thief is discovered. After all, I am not sorry it happened.

Elsie. Why, Will? Mother certainly thinks you a thief, so does Harry, and if father does not, he doesn't say so.

Will. But you *know* I'm not, and have promised that you will not marry any one else until I have been admitted to the bar.

Elsie. How could I refuse to promise that after what you did for my sake, Will?

Will. Are you quite sure that it is not gratitude instead of love, Elsie?

Elsie. I know it isn't. [*Rises.*] But I must go, dear. Mother will wonder what has become of me.

Will. If she suspected that you had been with me there would be a scene.

Elsie. Yes, she thinks she can make me marry Mr. Smarden, who wants to make use of my voice in his business. You should have seen his eyes snap when I refused to sing in the choir any more. He looked, for a moment, like a fiend.

Will. That man is either a lunatic or thoroughly bad. Either way he is dangerous, so have nothing to do with him. I feel certain he inspired that whitecapping episode last night. Shall I see you to-morrow?

Elsie. At the same place—till then, good-bye. [*Ex. L.*]

Ezra. [*Enters from saloon.*] Oh, Bill. [**Bill** *watching her off.*]

Will. Well, sir.

Ezra. [*Leaning c. against bench.*] I see you talkin' to my gal from the winder, yonder.

Will. Yes, I was speaking to her. [L. C.]

Ezra. Hain't ye got no more right feelin's than that, after what you done?

Will. I have done nothing that I'm ashamed of.

Ezra. You don't say so! Then all I have to say is that you hain't got no more shame than a naked statue. Why, you confessed yourself a robber, and give up the money.

Will. You are not quite correct. I didn't confess myself a thief, but I did give you the money. I said I restored your money, which had been taken under great temptation, and I was sorry the crime had been committed. I didn't say I took it.

Ezra. Same thing. Folks hain't givin' up two hundred and four dollars if they have a right to keep it these hard times, by gracious!

Will. Not as a general thing; but in this case I did.

Ezra. You don't say so. Oh, sho! You're coddin' me. [*Sits c.*]

Will. I was never more in earnest.

Ezra. What did you do it for?

Will. Because I'm in love with Elsie.

Ezra. That's natural. If I was a young feller, and no relation, be durned if I wouldn't git stuck on her, too. But what had that to do with the two hundred and four dollars?

Will. You suspected Harry, and so did I. She would break her heart if he were a thief, so to save her sorrow I took the blame.

Ezra. You don't say so! [*Jumps up.*] Then Harry did take it, after all.

Will. No, Harry did not take it. He is as innocent as I am.

Ezra. Then who did take it? Two hundred and four dollars can't unlock no cash box and fly away of their own accord. Somebody gobbled that money as sure as shooting. Who did it?

Will. That is just what I have set myself to find out, and if you will help me we will land the thief in jail before he is many hours older.

Ezra. By gracious, Bill, I'll do it. [*Shakes hands.*] I always liked you, and it kinder broke me all up when I thought you'd robbed me. I knew you had money saved, for you never spent none, and I like to see a young feller keerful sorter, hangin' onto the dollars.

Will. Say nothing to Mrs. Meeker or anybody about the matter, and don't be surprised if I pay you a visit.

Ezra. With Elsie to home? Well, I should say not! Oh, say, Bill, now that this thing is explained, hadn't you better gimme back them eighteen cents?

Will. Certainly. That will be two hundred and four dollars and thirty-two cents you owe me.

Ezra. You don't say so! Gosh durn it—I forgot I'd been robbed. Say, you'd better keep them eighteen cents, after all.

Will. All right, Mr. Meeker. If we don't catch the thief I'll never ask for my money. Then I may call and see Elsie? You have no objection to my attentions?

Ezra. Not a durn objection. Say, be durned if I wouldn't let you marry her jest to spite Mariar. I would, by gracious. [**Jaggsy** *sneaks on* R. 2 E.]

Jag. [*Aside.*] They say Lem's open agin. Now where's that dime? [*Searches pockets and finds it.*] Wow! here it is. [*Ex. into saloon.*]

Will. Then you have no reason for suspecting Lem Davis? [*Sits on bench with* **Ezra.**]

Ezra. Couldn't a been him, I tell ye. Why, I walked with him clear up town, and when I got back you was in the house, and so was Harry and Pickles.

Will. It is very perplexing. [**Pick.** *enters* L. I. E.]

Pick. Say, you hain't seen Pop no place? [*Leaning on back of bench.*]

Ezra. Why, no—hain't seen him to-day. What you want him for?

Pick. Miss Meeker says the saloon's open, and I know Pop's been workin' for Deacon Soper. I'm skeered he'll git peachy.

Ezra. Hain't sawn him. [*Noise in saloon and* Jag. *is thrown out by* Lem.] Jerusha! Here he is now.

Pick. Oh, Pop! Full again? [*Goes to him and helps him up.*]

Jag. Full of emptiness. Hain't broke *my* pledge—not much. [*Comes down* L.]

Ezra. What's the matter? Who threw you out?

Jag. Lem.

Ezra. What for?

Jag. Nothin'. I only went in to buy a little somethin' good for cramps, and he ordered me out. [L. C.]

Ezra. You don't say so. Throwin' stones at his own bar, by gracious.

Jag. He said he wouldn't serve no man that had jined the temperance, not if his tongue was hangin' out.

Ezra. You don't say so. [*Sits.*] Well, I reckon Lem's about right. When a man gits so low down 'at he can't control himself he'd ought to quit, and the liquor dealers ought to make him stay quit.

Jag. But I had the price.

Ezra. Don't make no difference. If Lem's goin' to stick to that rule they'll be a hull lot of folks in this town bringin' it in in original packages, and hidin' it under the sofy.

Pick. [L. *corner.*] Pop, I'm ashamed of you. First thing you know you'll be a regular old bum.

Ezra. Do you want to go to work?

Jag. Work? [*Recoiling in horror.*]

Ezra. So long since you did any you've forgot what it is, hey?

Jag. Oh, no; I've been helpin' the postmaster the last three days.

Ezra. Helpin' him how? As a horrible example at the temperance rallies?

Jag. No—runnin' errants for him.

Ezra. Well, if you want fifty cents a day and your keep for helpin' me out with my chores and stumpin' you can come along. But I'll hold back a week on ye, and if I ever smell liquor on your breath you lose that week's pay. I'm willin' to give any feller a show if he wants to quit, so now, John Hennery Thompson, brace up and be a man.

Will. You'd better take it, Jaggsy, while you have a chance. [*Leaning over bench.*]

Pick. [*Goes to him.*] Take it, Pop, please do. Mebbe after a while you and me can go to keepin' house and I won't have to be bound out to Mam Meeker by the county. Please take it, Pop—it's your last chance to git respectable.

Jag. Fifty cents a day and my keep and leave liquor alone? Them's pretty good wages for me, but I've sorter promised the Deacon I'd stop around in case he wanted me.

Pick. But this is a stiddy job, Pop.

Ezra. I reckon that's what hurts—he's been loafin' so long he hates to tackle anything stiddy, Haint got no sand in him.

Jag. Yes, I have, too. I was as likely a young feller as you was till you cut me out with Mariar Martin.

Ezra. [*Rises.*] John Hennery, that was the biggest durn fool trick I ever did, and you'd ought to thank your lucky stars I done it. You would if you'd had as much Mariar as I have. [*Goes* R.]

Jag. Mebbe you're right, Ezra. I'll take the job, anyhow—fifty cents a day and my keep and no liquor. But I'm on an errant for the Deacon now to Mr. Smarden. [*Lem enters from saloon. Buss of arranging kegs. Then leans against them. Has on apron.*]

Ezra. [R.] You let the Rev. Smarden rip and tend to me. I have no kinder use for that mis'ble coot, nor Seth Soper, neither. Anybody seen him to-day?

Jag. [L. C.] Why, I just come from him. He's feelin' awful bad.

Ezra. What's the matter of him?

Jag. Got a black eye, a game ankle and bruises all over. Says he fell down the sullar stairs last night.

Ezra. Ha, ha, ha, ho, ho, ho! Fell down the sullar stairs—oh, gosh! but that's good. He fell up agin his Uncle Ezra—that's what's the matter, and danced to the whistlin' of a blacksnake whip.

Lem. [*Loafing against bench.* **Will** *goes* R. *with* **Pick.**] He ain't the only one. Tom Barton says they was two other temperance galoots at the noon meetin' that looked as if they'd 'a' been drawed through a knothole.

Ezra. The next whitecap 'at tackles me 'll git drawed through a bunghole into a bar'l of tar. Now, say, Lem, I've hired John Hennery Thompson to work for me, and if you let him have any liquor you're goin to have your own troubles. Bill's goin' to Chicago putty soon, so he's quit me.

Lem. Too bad, ain't it? I thought he was goin' to stop here and run for mayor on the dry ticket. Thought he'd mebbe build a roof over the town with a steeple at one end and turn it into a Sunday school.

Will. When I do that I'll put you in as superintendent.

Ezra. And satan was there also. Eh, Bill?

Lem. [*Down* c.] Well, young feller, you're dead right to jump the town. The council has offered one hundred dollars reward for the arrest of the whitecap gang, and I calc'late you won't be the only reformer we'll have to lose.

Will. [*Hotly and threatening.*] If you mean that I was one of that fanatical crowd, you lie, and you know you lie.

Lem. Can't call liar at me. [*As he rushes at* **Will,** **Ezra** *gets between them.*]

Ezra. [*Backing him around stage.*] Well, of all the cantankerous, pepper-tempered, red-hot, all-fired, mean, ugly cusses I ever see, Lem Davis, you wear the belt. No matter what Bill Goodall thinks about the salcon, he's a man clear through to his boots. If he's got anything to say he'll say it clear to your face, and if he has any lickin' to do it'll be done by daylight like a man, not like a low-down sneakin' whelp in the dark of the moon.

Lem. [L.] If he wants some one to lick, I'm his man by daylight or dark. No white-livered, psalm-singin' prohibitionist can come monkeyin' around me callin' liar.

Will. You're a bully, and a sound drubbing would do you all the good in the world.

Ezra. [c.] Now, now Bill, don't make no muss. Lem's all right only for what ails him, and you're about the same. You're both good fellers in your way. Come, now, shake hands.

Will. I'll take the hand of no man I can't respect.

Lem. My sentiments to a dot. [*Begin to darken stage.*]

Ezra. You don't say so. Well, put your hands in your pockets. That'll keep you from scrappin' unless you use your feet. [Lem *retires up to saloon.*]

Pick. Come along, Dad, it's getting dark, and I'm not goin' to let you out after sundown. It's this night work that's killin' you.

Ezra. Yes—we'll all travel along to supper. Won't you come with us, Bill?

Will. No; thank you all the same, but I'd rather not.

Ezra. Well, so long. [*Going* L.] Come on, John Hennery. Don't you two git to makin' trouble agin or you'll hear from me. [*Ex* L. I. E.]

Pick. Come on, Pop. [*Pulling him* L.]

Jag. But that errant to Mr. Smarden, Gusta Ann.

Pick. Oh, shoot old Smarden. You come and git your supper. [*Ex. with* **Jag.** L. I. E.]

Lem. *Coming down to* **Will,** *who is sitting* c.] What you loafin' about here for?

Will. This is a free country, and I don't have to explain my business to you.

Lem. [L. C.] Don't hey? Well, you take my advice and keep away from my place.

Will. That's the best advice you've given in many a day. It's a pity your customers can't hear and act on it.

Lem. Are you goin' to move along?

Will. When I get good and ready.

Lem. All right. [*Ex. into saloon. Stage now dark. Lights showing in saloon.*]

Will. That fellow is very anxious to pick a fight. Perhaps it's just as well not to have trouble with him. He's an ignorant bully and there wouldn't be much glory in thrashing him. [*Ex. R. I. E. as* **Zach.** *enters* R. 2 E.]

Zach. So far all is well. Soper has sent me no word, so the expected letters have not arrived. [*Sits* C.] It now remains to be seen whether my will is strong enough to bring Mrs. Meeker here and compel her to do the deed. [*Takes off hat and rests head in hands.*] Come—I command it—I will it—come. [**Lem** *enters from saloon, sneaks up behind* **Zach.** *and strikes him over head with bungstarter.*]

Lem. Now will you move along. [**Zach.** *falls forward.* **Lem** *looks at him.*] Hello—what's this—the preacher! I've hit the wrong man. Smarden—Smarden I say! He doesn't answer—he's dead! Now I'm in a fix. Smarden—Smarden! [**Ezra** *enters* L. I. E.]

Ezra. What's the matter, Lem? Who is it?

Lem. I thought it was Bill, and gave him a soak on the head. I thought he was spying on me. It's Smarden!

Ezra. Say, Lem, this is serious.

Zach. Water—give me water.

Lem. Help me get him into the house and we'll soon bring him round. [*They support* **Zach.** *into saloon.*]

Mar. [*Enters* L. I. E.] Oh, you villains! Got the saloons runnin' full blast, hain't ye? Well, this'll be the last night of it in my propity. My conscience won't give me no peace night nor day as long's it's runnin', so here goes. [*Places dynamite and lights fuse in* L. 2 E.] Now, Lem Davis, and likewise Ezra Meeker, the judgment has come—you're come up with. [*Ex.* L. I. E.]

Will. [*Re-enters* R. *just as explosion takes place. Saloon breaks away, everything flips, bricks and mortar fall from trip board,* **Zach.** *and* **Lem** *fall through door,* **Ezra** *is pitched through window. Red fire. Fire bells heard.*]

Ezra. By gracious! You don't say so!

Curtain.

[*Second picture—*Will *under arrest by* Tom; Davis *pointing at him.* Mar. *and* Ezra *attending* Zach.]

ACT IV.

[*Same as Act II. At rise* Elsie *sewing at table* c. Harry *in armchair down* R. *reading.* Pickles *tidying room.*]

Har. [*Throwing down paper.*] It's no use, Sis, I can't read or anything else. I'm too worried and anxious.

Elsie. But why do you worry? Davis promised to let you have the money if he was allowed to reopen, and as he got permission he will no doubt keep his word.

Har. I wish I could feel sure of that, Sis. There's many a slip, you know, and if anything should occur to prevent him I shall be ruined.

Elsie. Will has not gone away yet—

Har. That thief—

Elsie. [*Rises.*] He is no thief—and if he were you should be the last to reproach him.

Har. I am rebuked, Sis. I beg your pardon.

Elsie. Will Goodall did not take that money. He thought you did, and gave up his own hard-earned savings to shield you.

Har. Nonsense—he confessed that he had taken it.

Elsie. He did not. He said the money had been taken under great temptation, and that he was sorry the crime had been committed—but he meant by you. He tried to save you for my sake.

Har. That may be all very well to tell you, Sis, for the purpose of gaining your favor, but it won't go down with me. Bill played a shrewd trick, and you were innocent enough to believe him.

Elsie. Harry Meeker! what base ingratitude—I am ashamed of you! [*Fire bell heard in distance.*]

Har. Hark! What's that?

Pick. It's a fire. [*Runs up to door and looks off.*] Oh, gee! somethin's afire just up street. The sky's all red—come—quick, quick and look at the smoke. [Har. *and* Elsie *go up and look off.*] I'll bet the whitecaps are burnin' down the town because they can't run it.

Elsie. How it burns! Oh, Harry, I'm afraid it will spread to us.

Har. No; the wind's in the wrong direction and, besides, there is plenty of water since the new pumps were put in.

Elsie. Why, who is this coming? Somebody has been hurt. It's mother—

Pick. With Lem Davis and Mr. Smarden. Gee, doesn't he walk wabbly—like a duck on a jamboree.

Elsie. Hush, Pickles. He has been injured. [*Lem and* **Mar.** *enter door in flat supporting* **Zach.** *He has head tied up.*]

Mar. Now then, Pickles, fly round and set that arm cheer. Elsie, you go and get a pillow and Harry, you help me take off his coat. How are you now, Brother Smarden?

Zach. In great pain and very faint, Sister Meeker.

Mar. We'll have you comfortable in a few minutes. Now, Harry, that arm is hurt. Careful how you pull. [*They take off coat.*] Go get me a basin of luke-warm water, Pickles. Elsie, I should think you might do somethin' when you see a feller creetur sufferin'. [**Pick.** *gets water, etc., from door* R. **Har.** *and* Lem *converse down* L.]

Elsie. What shall I do, mother?

Mar. Do? Why, get some cotton for bandages. You'll find the rag bag behind the door in the spare room. [*Ex.* **Elsie** L. I. E.]

Lem. [L. C.] It's a wonder we wa'n't all three killed.

Har. [L.] How did the explosion occur?

Lem. That's the pint we're after. Bill Goodall had been hangin' around the place for some time, and Joe Smith says he sold him dynamite and fulminatin' caps yesterday, so he was arrested on the spot.

Har. Bill was dead against the liquor traffic, too, but he didn't take an active part in the agitation on account of the old man's views.

Lem. More'n that—me and him had trouble twice. Well, I must hurry back. [*Going up.* **Elsie** *re-enters* L. I. E. *with bandages.*]

Har. Just one moment, Lem. I hope this won't make any difference to your loaning me the money?

Lem. I'm mighty sorry, but I couldn't do it nohow. You see, your dad's insured up to the last cent, so it don't matter to him; but my insurance ran out Monday and I didn't renew because I didn't know whether they was going to close me up or not. [*Going up.*]

Har. [*Following him.*] For heaven's sake, Lem, isn't there any way you could manage it?

Lem. No way at all—I lose everything. I'm sorry, but I can't let you take what I haven't got. [*Ex.* D. I. F. **Mar.** *is bathing* **Zach's** *wrist.*]

Har. [*Up* c. *Aside.*] My last hope is gone. Exposure is inevitable. [*Calls.*] Lem, Lem! [*Seizes hat and hurries off* D. I. F.]

Mar. How does that feel now, Brother Smarden?

Zach. Much easier, thank you.

Mar. [R. c.] That's good. Hustle and git me a needle and thread, Pickles, and you, Elsie, help me put on this bandage.

Elsie. [R.] Is the wound on your head very painful, Mr. Smarden? Will it need stitching?

Zach. I think not. The doctor said it was only a slight affair and that all it needed was bandaging.

Elsie. [*Looking at his arm.*] Why, what terrible bruises you have all up your arm. You must have been thrown against something with great force. They almost look like stripes from a whip.

Mar. You hush up, Elsie. Can't you see that Brother Smarden is in too much pain to be worried? How is it now? Any easier? Is that drawed too tight? Tell me if it hurts.

Zach. No, that will do nicely, Sister Meeker. I am much more comfortable already.

Mar. That's good. Now I'll go and make you a cup of strong tea. It's mighty comfortin', tea is, when you've been all shook up as you have.

Zach. Thanks, Sister Meeker. I think I could partake of a little tea. You are very good.

Mar. [*Aside. Going up.*] The good Lord knows I'd a cut my hand off rather than had this happen. [*Ex. door* R.]

Zach. It is at such a moment as this that a man feels the need of a wife, Miss Elsie. Some one to soothe his pain and sympathize with his misery. Don't you think so?

Elsie. [R. c.] Never having been a man, and in your position, I can scarcely offer an opinion, Mr. Smarden.

Zach. But you might be able to imagine how I feel.

Elsie. You are doubtless very nervous from the shock and in considerable pain.

Zach. Won't you please move that footstool a little to the right, Miss Elsie? [*She does so.*] Ah, thank you. Have you ever thought how important the lives of even the humblest of us may become when we are properly mated, Miss Elsie?

Elsie. I don't think I have ever considered the matter. [**Mar.** *re-enters unseen and listens.*]

Zach. You and I, for instance, are peculiarly fitted for each other.

Elsie. Do you think so? I fail to see it.

Zach. Indeed we are. Together we could do an immense

amount of good in temperance and evangelistic work.

Mar. [*Aside.*] He's agoin' to pop, and I'm agoin' to make her have him. That's why he ain't blamed me for blowin' him up along with the saloon, What a patient, long sufferin', Christian man he is!

Zach. My preaching, supplemented with your singing, something after the style of Moody and Sankey, might be made the means of saving thousands. Will you enter into a life partnership with me in the salvation of souls?

Elsie. No. [*After a pause.*]

Zach. You said——? [*Surprised.*]

Elsie. No—no, no! I hope you understand that I mean it. I wouldn't marry you, Mr. Smarden, under any consideration. [*Sits* c.]

Zach. But think of the life of ease and constant excitement. Our field would not even be bounded by America. England and foreign lands should be included in our vineyard. And as for money—the laborer is worthy of his hire, and all successful evangelists are handsomely remunerated.

Mar. [*Coming down.*] Ahem--excuse me—I couldn't help hearin' what you said, Brother Smarden. [*Hands him tea.*]

Zach. There is nothing to conceal, Sister Meeker. I am trying to induce Miss Elsie to become my wife.

Mar. Why, Elsie Meeker—you lucky gal! You'd ought to feel proud and happy for such a chance. Why, most gals 'ud jump at it.

Elsie. [c.] Then I'm not like most girls, mother. I have already told Mr. Smarden so, and that nothing could induce me to marry him.

Mar. Oh, sho! Just a young gal's whim. [*Aside to her.*] I'm sure Brother Smarden's a fine appearin' man and a powerful preacher. Why, you'd be the envy of every gal in town—yes, an' bigger towns'n this.

Elsie. I have no ambition to be envied in that way, mother. You know very well I have told you all along that I would never marry a man I didn't love, and I don't love Mr. Smarden. [*Ezra enters* D. I. F. *and comes down unseen.*]

Mar. Well, if you don't beat all I ever see! Ain't you ashamed to talk that way? Moreover, if you're thinkin' of Bill Goodall, I tell you pintedly that he's coolin' his heels in the lockup right now.

Ezra. You don't say so.

Mar. [*Crossing* L. *Aside.*] Durn that Ezra—he's allus got to poke his nose in jest when he's not wanted, and spile everythin'.

Elsie. [R. C.] What do you mean by saying Will is in the lockup?

Mar. They've took him for blowin' up the saloon and settin' it afire. Some of the folks was talkin' about lynchin' him, and the sheriff's goin' to take him to the county jail tonight.

Ezra. You don't say so. Well, for news. Mariar, you can give the Chicago papers pinters, by gracious.

Mar. [*Mocking.*] You don't say so.

Ezra. Yes I *do* say so. Bill Goodall didn't have nothin' to do with that business, as you and Smarden and Seth Soper well know. I signed his bonds myself, and they'll be mournin' in the temperance crowd afore this thing's done with.

Zach. You surely don't blame this to our people?

Ezra. Oh, no—no more'n I blame the whitecappin' last night. Reckon it must 'a' been Mariar, or Elsie here, or Pickles. We'll have to look out for them three desperate weemin. [*Retires up.*]

Zach. [*Aside.*] Then he does not suspect her. [*Aloud.*] Perhaps you think I struck myself with a slungshot, carried myself to the saloon and then exploded a bomb when I got inside.

Ezra. [*Up stage*] No, I don't nuther, 'cause I was there. [*Comes down* R.] But I do think you was waitin' for it to be did when you got clubbed, and that them as set it off didn't know you was inside. You fixed the cattridge and lit the fuse yourself for all I know.

Mar. [L. C.] Look out who you're accusin' Ezra Meeker. Don't you git the wrong pig by the ear or it'll make you trouble.

Ezra. You don't say so.

Mar. Lem Davis says Bill Goodall done it, and a man 'at'll steal two hundred and four dollars and fifty cents 'll do anythin'. He'd ought to be in the penitentiary on gineral principles, he had, if he *did* give it back.

Ezra. You don't say so. Don't you worry about the penitentiary, Mariar. They'll be some new faces in it before I drop this thing. [*Takes* C.]

Mar. It's a judgment, that's what it is, Ezra. It's a judgment onto you for flyin' in the face of Providence by maintainin' that saloon and ruinin' our boys and men with liquor. [*Crosses* R. *to* Zach.]

Ezra. [C.] Durn your judgments, Mariar. Durn your judgments, I say. This here business is fanatickism and crime, that's what it is, and it hain't no judgment whatsoever. What's more, I declare myself right now. I won't be bulldozed and I won't be driv. The temperance crowd has cost me mebbe a couple of thousan' dollars tonight but, by gracious, I'm agoin' to open three saloons to-morrer to show 'em that they can't skeer *me*. What's more, I'm goin' to put my name onto the signs.

Lem. [*Entering* D. I. F.] Good thing, Ezra, I'll help to push it along [*Comes down* L. C.] We've got enough stock to start 'em at that. There's three bar'ls of beer and five of whiskey and about nine cases of fine liquors. The cigars, though——

Ezra. I know—they all went up in smoke. How about fixtures?

Lem. Nothin' saved except the picture of Grover Cleveland. [*Or local character.*]

Ezra. You don't say so! Well, he was too tough to burn. Three bar'ls of beer, five of whiskey and some case liquors? I'll have them three saloons runnin' red hot before six o'clock to-morrer night. What you done with the stuff?

Lem. Moved it into the Dutchman's basement and Harry's attendin' to it.

Mar. [R. *leaning on armchair.*] My boy 'tendin' to a stock of liquor? Oh, Brother Smarden, that I should ever have lived to see this day. [*Sobbing. Kneels by armchair.*]

Ezra. Mariar Meeker, don't make a fool of yourself—nature has did enough for you in that line. It hain't agoin' to hurt Harry no more'n it's hurt me.

Zach. "At the last it biteth like a serpent and stingeth like an adder."

Ezra. Hain't never stung me none. I don't know the taste of it, so I never had the snakes bitin' and stingin' me.

Zach. Sister Meeker, I am afraid my arm is swelling. The bandage grows uncomfortably tight.

Mar. Then I'll loosen it. [*Buss.*] Why, it *is* swole up a hull lot.

Ezra. What's the matter? Sprained or broke? [*Going* R.]

Zach. Sprained, I think. [**Mar.** *has bandage off.*]

Ezra. Say, parson, what's all them black and blue marks?

Zach. [*Trying to pull down shirt sleeve.*] I contracted those bruises when I fell. They are most painful.

Ezra. You don't say so. I never see bruises turn black so quick. Reckon your fall was a good deal like Seth Soper's. He fell down the sullar stairs last night. Shouldn't wonder if you have wales on your back as big's my finger, and if them ain't whip-lash marks I'll be switched.

Zach. What do you mean?

Ezra. That there's a hundred dollars reward out for the white-cap gang, and I know the names of two of 'em. [*Crossing* L.] Oh, I'll teach some folks to be careful how they monkey with their Uncle Ezra. [**Will** *enters* D. I. F. *Goes to* **Elsie** L.] Hello, Bill.

Will. I said I'd see you this evening.

Mar. Well, of all the nerve, Bill Goodall! How dast you come here, after what you done last night?

Will. [L.] Mr. Meeker invited me.

Mar. Well, it's all accordin' to taste. Ezra may not hold himself above mixin' up with a thief, but I do. [*Turns her back.*]

Zach. So do I, Sister Meeker, so do I. If you will assist me, I think I am able now to get home.

Ezra. Don't see no rope tyin' you, if you're bent on goin'.

Mar. [R. C.] Don't you insult my company, Ezra Meeker—I won't stand it. [*Goes R. of arm chair.*]

Ezra. You don't say so. [*Crosses R. and places a chair.*] Mebbe you'll take a chair and sit it. [*Retires up a little.*]

Will. [L. C.] Before you go, Mr. Smarden, I'd like to ask you a few questions, if you have no objection. [*Takes C.*]

Zach. Certainly not, if they are proper ones.

Will. [C.] They are perfectly proper, but I warn you that your answers will have to be scrupulously accurate. What hold have you over Postmaster Soper? [**Lem** *and* **Elsie** L. *listening.*]

Zach. Hold? Why, none.

Will. Then is there any reason why he should violate the postal laws in your interest?

Zach. I don't see what you mean.

Will. Soper, at your instigation, has intercepted letters addressed to another person and sent them to you. That is a penitentiary offense.

Zach. I know nothing about it. I never received any other person's letters.

Will. No—because Jaggsy has confessed all and handed over the letters to me. Here they are. These are your property, Lem Davis. [**Lem** *takes letters and opens them.* **Mar.** *assists* **Zach.** *to rise and begins to help him on with his coat.*]

Lem. What's your hurry, Smarden? Don't tear yourself away.

Zach. I have a duty to perform. As a good citizen I am going to get a warrant for the man who committed a brutal and unprovoked assault.

Ezra. You don't say so.

Lem. [L. C.] What name are you goin' to sign to it? Better make it James Cooke or you are liable to have trouble yourself for perjury.

Zach. Slanderer.

Lem. Read that, Ezra. [*Gives him letter.*]

Ezra. [c. *Reads.*] "In answer to your inquiry, I never heard of any such person as Zachariah Smarden. A man answering to your description, and calling himself Cooke, conducted a temperance revival here, but left suddenly after borrowing considerable money." Elmer Gizzard—no, not Gizzard—Blizzard—no, it's Vizzard. Why does folks want to sign their names so nobody can't read 'em?

Lem. Here's another. Read that.

Ezra. [*Reads.*] "Zachariah Smarden conducted a temperance revival here some weeks ago, and several of our best people would like to see him from five to ten dollars worth. We have since heard that he served a term at Fort Madison under a different name. [*Signed*] Aminadab Johnson." What you got to say to that?

Zach. Only that those letters are forgeries and part of a conspiracy to blacken my character. I shall not stay here to be insulted any longer. [*As he is getting on his coat wallet falls on floor.* **Pick.** *picks it up and he puts it in breast pocket of coat.*]

Pick. [*Who has been up stage. Handing wallet.*] Here, mister, you don't want to forget this. Oh, yes—there's something else of yours here. [*Ex. r. 1. e. returning at once with umbrella.*]

Ezra. [*Rising, goes c*] Where there's smoke there's fire. Folks hain't *all* slanderin' one poor innocent man. No, by gracious!

Pick. [r. c.] *Hiding umbrella behind her.*] Did you lose anything here last night, mister?

Zach. I have not missed anything.

Pick. Finders keepers, losers seekers?

Zach. First tell me what it is.

Pick. An umbrella. Prove your property and you can have it.

Ezra. He didn't lose no umbrel', 'cause he was just goin' without it when I picked it up and called attention to it.

Mar. [r.] And I handed it to him. It hain't Brother Smarden's umbrel', Pickles.

Pick. [*Showing it.*] Hain't eh? Then what's it got his name on it for? There it is, as plain as a pancake.

Ezra. You don't say so. Well, by gracious! [*Takes umbrella, looks at it, pauses, drops it, grabs* **Zach.** *and takes wallet from his pocket.*]

Zach. Here, stop that! What are you doing?

Ezra. Lookin' for two hundred and four dollars and fifty cents that some sneak thief stole from me last night. [*Opens wallet, takes out money, counts it.*] And I've got it to the last cent.

Mariar, it's all accordin' to taste. You may not be above mixin'
up with a thief, but I am. [C.]

Zach. [R. C.] Give me back that wallet and the money, too;
they are both mine.

Ezra. You don't say so. Lem, is they any way you can recog-
nize the money you paid me last night? Can you remember what
notes they was?

Lem. There was a corner torn off a five dollar note and a ten
spot was torn in two near the middle. I mended it myself with
gum paper.

Will. [L. *with* Elsie.] If you find those two notes the money
is identified.

Zach. [Ezra *searching through roll.*] You'll never find them.

Ezra. You don't say so. Well, there's the ten spot, just as
Lem said, and here's the fiver, by gracious. Bill, here's your
money—count it and see if it's all O. K. [*Gives* Will *money.*]

Will. [*To* Elsie. *Aside.*] Harry shall have the two hundred
dollars after all.

Ezra. Now, you mis'ble, ornery, thievin' fraud, what you got
to say for yourself? [*Crossing* R.]

Zach. Nothing. [*Calmly.*]

Ezra. Nary a word, eh? Suppose you're a poor, innocent man
'at hasn't been give no show, hain't ye? You're not guilty—
oh, no!

Zach. Oh, yes. I took the money. I opened the cash box
with that key. [*Shows key.*]

Ezra. You don't say so! You hain't got a single lie left in
stock, have ye?

Zach. Not one that would do any good. That evidence would
convict.

Ezra. Convict? Well, you bet your boardin' house it will.
I'm afraid you won't find it right comfortable in jail tonight, but
I got to send you there. I hope you'll excuse me, Brother Smar-
den.

Zach. Don't apologize, Brother Meeker. I don't intend to go
to jail.

Ezra. You don't say so! How do you propose to keep out
Brother Smarden?

Zach. By insisting that if I go, dear Sister Meeker shall keep
me company.

Ezra. Mariar? What's Mariar been doin'?

Zach. [*Rises.*] Committing arson, incendiarism or something
like that, by blowing up your building tonight and almost doing
murder. She confessed to me after it was done, and told me,
when and where she got the dynamite.

Ezra. [*Aside.*] Mariar? By gracious, this is the worst blowin' up she's give me in thirty years. [*Aloud.*] Was this you doin's Mariar?

Mar. [*Crosses to him* c.] It's true, Ezra. I done it, but I thought I was doin' right. That wicked wretch had me so worked up overgittin' rid of the saloon that I couldn't rest. He said it was the Lord's work, and that I could claim the buildin' as my thirds, and that I had a right to blow it up if I wanted. But my eyes is opened now—the spell is off me and if you want to send me to jail I'm willin'—I deserve it.

Ezra. You don't say so!

Mar. Yes, I *do* say so. [*Crying.*] I've been a wicked woman as well as a durn fool.

Ezra. You have, Mariar, you have.

Mar. I hain't treated you right, Ezra. I know I hain't, and the children'll grow up to be ashamed of their mother.

Ezra. They will, Mariar, because you're guilty of the crime of arsenic. [**Har.** *enters* D. I. F. *drunk. Carries red-handled fireman's ax over shoulder.*]

Har. [*Staggering down* L. C.] Hello, ole man. Whee! Great time—great time.

Ezra. Why, son—what's the matter?

Har. [L. C.] Never had so much fun—hic—in my life. Opened saloon in Dutchman's basement and treated all—hic—the boys. The boys all treated me—hic—and now they're all treating themselves. [**Elsie** *crying on* **Will's** *shoulder* L.]

Ezra. [C.] Mariar—we've been a pair of durn fools. [*Grabs* **Zach.** *and runs him out* D. I. F. *Comes down.*] There's the first act of ginuine reform. We've been a pair of durn fools, and if you'll forgive me for that [*pointing to* **Harry**], I'll forgive you. Bill, you take care of Elsie—for good and all if you want to—and, Mariar, you put that fool boy to bed. Gimme that ax. [*To* **Har.** L. C.]

Mar. [R. C.] What are you goin' to do, Ezra?

Ezra. [C.] I'm goin' to bust up all that's left of three bar'ls of beer, five bar'ls of whiskey and nine cases of fine liquors. I'm goin' to spill 'em in the sewer, where they belong, and if anybody asks you, just tell 'em that Uncle Ezra Meeker is right on the temperance question and dead agin the saloon.

Curtain.

		Harry. Lem.
Mar.	**Ezra.**	
Pickles.		**Elsie. Will.**

www.ingramcontent.com/pod-product-compliance
Lightning Source LLC
Chambersburg PA
CBHW030717110426
42739CB00030B/725